Knock Out Your Debt

Arm Yourself for the Battle Against Debt

by

Steve Kenworthy

authorHOUSE™

1663 Liberty Drive, Suite 200
Bloomington, Indiana 47403
(800) 839-8640
www.AuthorHouse.com

First published by AuthorHouse 05/25/05

ISBN: 1-4208-5188-8 (sc)

Library of Congress Control Number: 2005903769

Printed in the United States of America
Bloomington, Indiana

This book is printed on acid-free paper.

These materials have been developed to teach, educate, and help individuals and families how to understand the fundamentals of money, debt, and credit.

The author has compiled much of the information from years of personal experiences He continuously teaches the public proper money management. Steve has done thousands of consultations and seminars throughout the country.

Information was also obtained from CitiBank, Wall Street Journal, Business Weekly, NFCE, Federal Trade Commission, Equifax, Experian, and TransUnion, Money Magazine and Consumer Reports.

Special Dedication To Two Very Special Women In My Life

My Mother, Monique Marie Therese Alic-Tuquat Kenworthy, who went to heaven when I was nine years old. I know you are always nearby, watching over me. We will be together again someday.

My Sister, Jaqueline (Hafner) Kenworthy, who passed away November 11th, 2005 before I could complete my book. I hope you are proud of me. I miss you very much.

Knock Out Your Debt

Your complete guide to financial peace of mind through proper money management.

Please do not ever forget: What your mind conceives and believes, you can achieve!

A note from the author, Steve Kenworthy

Congratulations for receiving and reading this book. **It will change your life financially for the better.** I am blessed to be in a profession that helps individuals no matter where in the U.S. they might live. The strategies in this book can and will make your life financially better, but it is not up to me. All I can do is put the time-tested and proven words on paper. It is up to you to take action. Having presented thousands of Financial Education Seminars for employees for some of the largest companies in the United States, taught in high schools and colleges, made radio and television appearances, and written financial newsletters, I speak from experience when I say THIS WORKS. I know finances are not on most people's Top Ten list of things to read or think about, maybe not even in the top one hundred. In my opinion, there are not many things that are as important as your financial future. It affects not only you, but also your family. Who are we all accountable for? Ourselves. Everyone has his/her own story and more often than not, several. Life can be and usually is very challenging at times. I was very fortunate to be raised in an environment that taught our family that we can do or be anything we want as long as we believe in ourselves and do not give up when things get tough. Always treat people the way you would like to be treated, have a game plan, a sincere desire, confidence, a commitment to accomplish your dreams and goals, and do not let **anyone** hold you back. I not only learned important life lessons from my parents, I also live by them.

I do not know anyone, who, after a tragedy or major setback, in his or her life, did not have to deal with the fallout of that experience. Most of us have made big mistakes that knocked us off our feet. The hardest thing is to get up and keep going. I personally have fallen flat on my face several times and didn't think I would ever recuperate. My mother passed away when I was only nine years old. I was hit with an unexpected divorce I never saw coming. Being unable to see my children everyday caused me not to care about anything. I lost my job, friends, pride, self-esteem, confidence, material things and much more. There was a time when the only place I had to live was inside my car. My only other possessions were a few clothes and a 19-inch television. I had the attitude of giving up and not caring anymore, even after everything we, as a family, were taught and practiced on a daily basis.

Everyone needs help from time to time. Using help from family, friends, teachers, preachers and co-workers are all good places to start the rebuilding process. Needless to say, I got back on my feet and it feels great! Anyone can do it with motivation, a belief in oneself, determination, patience, a never-give-up attitude, and the right game plan. We have to create our own plan. That is what this book is about, getting you on the right path to Financial Peace Of Mind. As the commercial says, that is priceless. Surround yourself with positive people and avoid negative individuals. They will bring you down very quickly. I have had the pleasure of meeting thousands of individuals over the years, and do you know what I discovered? We all have goals and dreams. Making them a reality is up to you. Successful people are willing to do things other people are not willing to do. It is honestly that simple. What the mind conceives and believes, it can achieve.

Being raised in the old school, I was taught that a man's word is his bond. I give you my word, if you follow the advice and strategies in this book, **YOU WILL BE SUCCESSFUL!** Will it be easy? Not always. Is it worth the reward? Absolutely! Please do not attempt to take short cuts. There are none. When you make something that requires a recipe, what would happen if you left out some ingredients? How long would any company stay in business without an accounts payable/accounts receivable department? Not very long. This book is your plan to stay in business as a family. **Dare to dream!** I know you have heard this too many times, but if I can do this, you can too. Again, it is up to you. Please do not sell yourself short. Make this a positive, proud and defining moment in your life. I promise that you will relish the financial peace of mind.

Finally, please teach your children about finances. Do not let your children stub their toes as often as we have because there was nowhere to learn about finances and proper, money management skills. They deserve better and often depend on their parents for guidance and support. That is our job and duty as loving parents. I am sadly shocked when I teach young adults in schools and colleges. They have no idea of money management and basic financial practices. None what-so-ever! Whose responsibility is it to teach our children the things they might not learn in school? I believe the answer is obvious. This book is intended for the entire family. After reading and putting the advice and strategies into practice, you will know 95% more about finances than most other individuals. Over time, your financial situation will steadily improve. You can do this. Thousands of people before you already have. Why not you? **Believe.**

Wishing you and yours the best success.

Your Complete Guide To Financial Peace Of Mind Through Proper Money Management

The most important step to realizing your dream of Financial Peace of Mind is to **START** **TODAY.** Please do not allow procrastination to keep you from fulfilling your hopes, dreams, and a secure future for your family. The information contained in this book does work and will guide you to the type of lifestyle you deserve and have worked so hard to attain. Your success depends on several things; commitment, taking action, and **a sincere desire to make thinking changes, lifestyle changes and priority changes.** Many people try to solve money problems with money, but that does not and will not work. Being in the profession of helping the public with their finances and speaking to 10's of thousands of families throughout the country, I have witnessed success time and time again by people just like yourself who follow the strategies and information compiled in this book. I believe all of us reach a point where we say, **"enough is enough"**, so together, let us make **today** the day your financial challenges, debt and the stress that comes with it will be eliminated. Always do your very best and you will win.

Facts

According to The American Bar Association, 89% of all divorces are directly related to finances.

Debt is the number one reason for a lack of an adequate retirement fund.

The average American spends less than 24 hours in their entire lifetime planning for retirement.

Debt is the number one cause of stress and anxiety, which over time, will affect your health.

71% of families are near or at financial crisis.

Debt is a major factor in excessive absenteeism, lack of job productivity and job performance.

Bankruptcies exceeded 1.5 million in 2003. One every 15 seconds!

Consumer debt is at an all time high of over 1.4 trillion dollars.

People, who solely rely on Social Security are struggling on a daily basis.

Senior citizens use of credit cards has gone up 90% in the past 10 years.

Most people have less than two weeks savings in case of an unexpected emergency.

How Many Of The Following Apply To Yourself Or Someone You Know?

Are your debts making your home life unhappy?

Are you at, or very near your credit limits?

Does debt pressure divert your attention from your job?

Do your debts cause you to think less of yourself?

Do you pay only minimum payments on your accounts?

Have you made unrealistic promises to your creditors

Are you thinking about borrowing money to pay off your debts?

Do creditors harass you regarding late payments?

Do you fear family and friends will discover your debt?

Have you borrowed money with high interest rates?

Have you taken cash payments from one card to pay another?

Do the payments that you are making fail to lower the debt?

Are you paying high finance charges?

Are late fees added to your statements?

Do you wonder how you will pay the next bill or bills?

Do you take out "pay day loans"?

If you answered yes to more than 5-9, you are rapidly approaching debt crisis.
If you answered yes to 10 or more, you are probably in a serious debt crisis.

Chapter 1—Taking Control of Your Finances

Chapter One will review the importance of getting your finances organized with extreme effectiveness.

With knowledge, commitment and self-control, anyone can become a magnet for financial opportunity—instead of being a victim of continual financial crisis. Planning for financial wellness requires making the best decisions and choices on how to spend your money. Most people assume that if you make more money, you will have more money. This is not true at all. Many people who are being helped by a consumer credit counseling agency, or debt management organization, earn in excess of $250,000 per year, and come from all walks of life. Poor spending habits, regardless of your income, can almost guarantee accruing overwhelming debt. Having financial peace of mind and control of your finances requires lifestyle changes, thinking changes, priority changes and, most importantly, proper financial planning and a sincere desire to make appropriate changes. Some very difficult sacrifices and work will be required. But, you can join tens of thousands of consumers who are taking charge of their finances. Join this challenge and experience the excitement of achieving financial peace of mind!

Setting Financial Goals

Unless you plan on winning the lottery or inheriting a lot of money, developing financial goals is crucial and requires proper planning. You must have patience, discipline, and a sincere willingness and desire to accomplish your financial goals. There are basically three different types of goals, each being equally important.

• Short-Term Goals

Goals you will accomplish in one month to one year.

Most people are willing to cut out some luxury items and services for short periods of time in order to achieve identifiable, short-term goals that build toward financial freedom. You will gain confidence and motivation when you break down a problem into do-able outcomes. Achievement of short-term financial goals fosters a sense of power over problems that can seem insurmountable. Are there any luxury items you can eliminate? Make a list of goals—with specific target dates—that you will reach in one month to one year.

• Mid-Term Goals

Goals you will accomplish in one to five years.

It is impossible to achieve true financial wellness without a destination in mind. You cannot know where you are going or if you are already there, unless you have a definable destination (your goal). Having a vision of mid-term goals will help you stay on the plan. Mid-term goals might be eliminating all of your credit card debt, participating in a retirement plan, buying a car, building a sizeable emergency fund, taking your family on a nice vacation you have only been able to fantasize about, and whatever else you can imagine. Always have a dream.

• **Long-Term Goals**

<u>Goals you will accomplish in five years or longer.</u>

THE BIG PICTURE! Whether you want to own your own home, create substantial savings, provide for a comfortable retirement nest egg to live the lifestyle you desire and deserve, or pay for your child's education, effective financial planning requires a <u>long-range</u> perspective.

1. Commit your goals in **writing**. This will allow you to realize your financial dreams.

2. Be very specific and realistic in identifying your goals.

3. Give yourself a timeframe to accomplish each goal.

4. **Believe in yourself**—that you will accomplish the goal.

5. You must have a sincere desire to accomplish the goal.

6. Your goals will change from time to time, so be flexible.

7. DO NOT LET ANYONE rain on your parade.

8. Review your goals after three months and monitor your progress toward these goals.

9. As an enhancement to your goals, create a dreams list.

10. Reward yourself when you accomplish a goal. This is very important.

11. Successful individuals are willing to do things that others are not willing to do.

IMPORTANT Steps To Take For Proper Goal Planning

1. Determine a specific goal you want to accomplish. Stay unswervingly dedicated to achieving this goal. Stay focused, which may be difficult at times. Sometimes the best-laid plans do not go as planned. Get

your whole family involved. Many children and young adults have no idea about the outside world. We should prepare them to understand finances. If we do not, who will? Reading this book will give them a wealth of practical information regarding their financial future.

2. Develop a specific game plan to achieve your goals. Determine the timeframe to complete each goal. Monitor your progress frequently. Organize your activity and maintain your enthusiasm. Roll with the punches. Review your goals every three months. (You may need to adjust your goals from time to time.) Patience is an important element in getting results. Financial challenges will not change overnight. This complete process is not a get-rich-quick program.

3. Have a sincere, burning desire to attain the things you want in life—nothing less! There is a big difference between a wish and a goal. Recognize the difference, but remember that your opportunities are endless. Once you get into the habit of success, the rewards will be amazing and self-gratifying. You can do this! Having strong willpower will not be enough for you to succeed. Willpower fades with time. You must have the sincere desire and commitment.

4. Develop extreme confidence about yourself and your abilities. Do not accept the possibility of defeat. Never give up! Concentrate strictly on the positive and your strengths. Sometimes we forget all the good things we have done in life, and negative events will normally overshadow the positive ones. Get yourself a pad and start writing all the positive things you have accomplished in your life. Do not consider anything too small or of little importance. Your list is pretty impressive, isn't it? Concentrate on the positives.

5. Do not allow criticism, what others might say, circumstances, or any obstacle affect your dogged determination to succeed. Often and unknowingly, individuals whom we share our lives with think they know what is better for us than we, ourselves, do. Do not let anyone rain on your parade to a better financial destination. Opportunities

come to those who go after them, not those who wait. Develop a dogged determination to follow through on YOUR plan. We are accountable to ourselves.

6. "Successful people are the ones willing to do things that others are not willing to do." You will read this phrase several times in this book, and it is really that simple.

I cannot stress enough the importance of setting goals for getting where you want to be. Reading how to do it is not going to be as easy as taking action. I promise you, continuously applying these steps will become second nature to you. Action and consistency will create the desired results. Your financial situation will change for the better. Over time, correctly managing your finances will become exciting, as you create a bright future. Seeing the light at the end of the tunnel is strictly up to you. Remember: YOU CAN DO THIS! I wish you could see, through my eyes, the great things awaiting you. There are so many goal opportunities in this book. Highlight them as you read. START NOW and create "Your Personal Success Plan."

Suggested goals

Start today!
Read this book.
Highlight areas in the book that are of importance to you.
Keep track of your spending.
Order copies of your credit report(s).
Create a total game plan for yourself.
Calculate your Debt-to-Income Ratio.
Protect yourself against identity theft.
Prepare a budget.
Write down your goals.
Eliminate credit card debt.
Negotiate reducing your credit card interest rates.

Start a savings plan.
Correct errors in your credit files.
Contribute more to your company-sponsored retirement plan.
Take advantage of an employer-matching plan.
Dare to dream.
BELIEVE IN YOURSELF!

The goal possibilities are endless. The tools for reaching these goals are in your hands.

Budgeting

A household budget is a financial statement of estimated income and expenses for an individual or family for a selected period of time. How long do you think a company or an organization, regardless of its size and success, would be in business without an accounts payable and an accounts receivable department? A budget is our necessary accounts payable/accounts receivable department. It ensures personal financial stability in a society where we buy now and pay later. More than 1.5 million consumers filed for personal bankruptcy in 2004—one every fifteen seconds. A budget would have prevented the need to go through this process.

Budget analysis begins by gathering all facts. Track down where all the money consistently goes. This is like detective work—you need evidence that can come in the form of writing down every penny you spend for at least one month. Use pay stubs, cancelled checks, cash expenditures, receipts, and credit card statements. The purpose of budgeting is to be certain your monthly expenses do not exceed your monthly net income. Take control of your spending. Know for a FACT that proper budgeting will overcome most financial challenges.

According to the U.S. Census Bureau, consumer debt has reached $1.4 trillion. Now is the time to discover where all your money is going: Cellular phones, cable television, luxury items, entertainment, groceries, movies, mortgage or rent, tobacco, dining out often, hobbies, utilities, frequent fast-food stops, healthcare and medication costs, magazine subscriptions, excessive spending (living beyond your means). The list goes on and on—too many even to begin to list. The worst expense of all is unexpected emergencies, usually bad news that will cost you money—often times, more money than you have. Start saving. Begin striving for financial peace of mind now, this very moment.

START TODAY!

Many consumers fail to take the most difficult step—taking the first step. Sometimes finances can be intimidating because we are afraid of what the bottom line will look like. We tend to ignore the big picture. Take one day at a time. You WILL succeed! Decide to make a positive change regarding your finances today. Do not let procrastination, embarrassment, or fear keep you from bettering your own and your family's life. "We are where we are," and "bad things do happen to good people," but it is up to you and your family to say "enough is enough" and take action now.

The information contained in this book will put you back on the right path and allow you to see the light at the end of the tunnel. Keep in mind, life is not a sprint, but a marathon. Be patient and never give up! I have had the privilege and honor of advising consumers just like you for almost twenty years, and I receive countless thanks from clients—letters, cards, phone calls and e-mails. THIS PLAN WORKS!

Start by calculating all of your income. List your total expenses and separate them into **essentials and non-essentials.** (See examples below.) Whatever amount of time and effort are required in order for you to be prepared financially is well worth it. Believe it or not, getting to your financial destination will become fun after awhile, although it will get rough from time to time. Hit an obstacle, think and find a way to conquer it. There will be more than one. Do not get discouraged or give up. Keep taking positive steps toward your goals. Over time, you will feel more empowered—a great feeling to have over money.

Essentials

Essential Items are food, shelter and clothing, and expenses that cannot be altered, such as medications, utilities, childcare costs, and insurance, products and services that are a "must" to have.

Non-essentials

Non-essential items can be targeted for adjustments or elimination, such as cellular telephones, cable television, magazine subscriptions, entertainment, dining out, and unnecessary services. Challenge EVERYTHING in your spending patterns and look for places to cut back and save. Did you know that many people spend more money dining out than they do buying groceries? By making a budget and identifying your spending patterns, you will be very surprised where your hard-earned money is disappearing. Later on, we will give you several ways to save and find hidden money. Following these strategies will save you 15% to 20% of your spending without making any noticeable changes to your lifestyle. Did I forget to mention the part about certain sacrifices? You must be willing to make a sacrifice here and there. Life involves making very tough choices. Giving up some non-essential items will not be easy. What are your priorities? You must make choices.

Top Sources of Debt

1. Easy access to credit. There are more than 1 billion credit cards in use today and, according to Citibank, more than 2.5 billion solicitations are mailed to every sector of society each year. That number is almost unimaginable. 2.5 BILLION solicitations! Eliminate the urge to respond to them by calling the 800 number for "The Opt Out Option" (mentioned later), which eliminates new credit card offers from being sent to you for a period of time.

2. Easy access to money. ATM/debit cards make it certain that you will **ALWAYS** spend more! Leave them home more often and use cash only.

3. The consumer culture. Americans are increasingly becoming media-driven in trying to keep up with television personalities, instead of with the Jones'. WHY? Many Americans confuse ownership of material things with success. Success does not mean owning a bunch of stuff that you probably still haven't paid for.

4. Changing technology. Many Americans are susceptible to advertising for big-ticket items, such as computers, which appear to be absolutely necessary in our fast-paced society. New hi-tech features in cars, household appliances, and wireless communications increase what consumers pay for these products. There is even a $40 product that will remove lids from your jars. Thank you very much! I do have a new $40 gadget, which I HAD to have, but since owning this remarkable breakthrough product, I have used it twice in two years. It was an emotional decision for a non-essential product, a waste of money. Buyer's remorse, "What was I thinking?" is the only thing going through my mind. Don't cave in to pressure; make the right choice. You will save thousands and thousands of dollars. Just say "no" to yourself more often when you are facing a buying decision. It's easy...NOT always, but you CAN say no!

5. Lack of financial education and literacy. Most individuals are not pro-active in the management of their money. In other words, most Americans do not know much about money. Money buys things, but it's about a lot more than that. You have a great opportunity to start acting on the information in this book. Start today.

ACTION + KNOWLEDGE = POWER

Successful people are willing to do things others are not willing to do. This book will give you a jumpstart and a designed track to run on regarding your personal finances. Remember, IT WORKS! There is a light at the end of the tunnel. You have my word, but you may have to leave your comfort zone for awhile.

6. Financial setbacks. Loss of income, disability, medical emergency, death in the family, overtime hours eliminated can set you back on your financial heels. We need adequate savings for such circumstances, but we no longer save like we did in the 70s and mid 90s. The average American saves 0.04% of his/her income and spends less than twenty-four hours **in a lifetime** preparing for their retirement. How is that working?

7. Over spending and living beyond your means. Many over-spenders rationalize their spending by imagining that their income will increase. Advertisers prey on this assumption by offering "no payments until next year" programs, 0% interest, and no money down. The same happens at tax refund time. Businesses offer to allow you to use your tax refund even before you receive it, so that you can buy their product. Own it now, and pay later. What a deal! Think about it first. Do you really need it? Make wise choices.

Control Spending

Emotions and impulses play a very big part in your spending habits. The most effective way to control your spending is to **KEEP TRACK OF EVERY PENNY YOU SPEND!** Have you ever started Monday with $20 in your pocket and by Wednesday you have only $1.73 left? Where did it go? Or do you rationalize that you make A, spend B and should have C left over—but amazingly, the difference, C, is rarely there. This strategy of keeping track of every penny you spend can be somewhat demanding and cumbersome. It will also tax your willingness to change and step out of your financial comfort zone. **Please, please do this exercise.** I promise, you will be amazed when you find out where and how your money is being spent. Knowledge is power. Knowing exactly where you are spending your money will allow you to change your spending patterns. Identifying your spending habits will allow you to cut back on unnecessary purchases. This exercise will help you decide what you need and don't need. **Sixty five percent** of all purchases we make are **unplanned!** SIXTY FIVE PERCENT! Work on saying no to yourself more often. Leave your debit and credit cards at home and just use cash. When you shop, take someone with you with the understanding that he/she will help you from buying something based on emotions, instead of an informed choice. Avoid buyer's remorse. Think before buying a big ticket item (car, stereo system, computer, appliance) and wait 3-5 days. You may come to the realization that you really don't NEED it. This is probably the most important exercise in this book.

I cannot stress enough the importance of knowing exactly where you are spending your money. Budgeting is the most effective way to accomplish that. Designate who will take charge of your family's accounts payable/accounts receivable department, just as a business does. What would happen to any business that does not maintain accounts payable/accounts receivable? Nothing good! The business is guaranteed to fail. You CAN succeed! **KEEP TRACK OF EVERY**

PENNY YOU SPEND FOR AT LEAST ONE MONTH! I cannot overstate the importance of completing this exercise. We have had clients and prospects "find" as much as $1,500 per month that they had no idea they were spending. That is enough money to use for contributing to a retirement plan, such as a Roth IRA. Don't let your money disappear into a black hole.

Where is **your** money going? Find out! You will get excited when you discover where your hard-earned money is going and what expenses you might be able to eliminate in order to increase your monthly cash flow. Think of it as giving yourself a raise—a well-deserved raise.

The Impact Of Debt

According to the American Bar Association, 89 % of all divorces are directly related to debt problems.

The number one reason people have **inadequate retirement funds is too much debt.**

Debt is one of the main causeS of stress and anxiety, which can lead to poor health over time.

37% of employees are near financial crisis (robbing Peter to pay Paul), and 34% are in financial crisis (robbing Peter **and** Paul).

Debt is a major factor in excessive job absenteeism, lack of job productivity, and job performance, which affects a company's bottom line). Employees find it difficult to focus on other things, such as their job responsibilities, while they are dealing with excessive debt and the constant thoughts as to how they can pay the debt. This situation is very stressful for anyone.

Money = Happiness

No! Having plenty of money does not guarantee happiness. The love of money may be the root of all evil, but it also makes the world go 'round. How would you prefer your world to go around? Pause for a moment and ask yourself, "What would my financial picture look like if I did everything exactly as I did last year? Would your financial situation be the same, worse, or better? Do you know that most lottery winners spend ALL their winnings within three years? It is WHAT you do with your money, not HOW much money you have. Many Americans seem to have evolved into a generation that believes having a lot of stuff is equivalent to being successful. At the end of the day, it is still stuff. Do you know anyone who lives in a fancy, $400,000 house, but cannot afford any furnishings, because their borrowing power is maxed out? We do. Make the right choices. Think about it! Talk about it! Then, make informed buying decisions.

Important Saving Suggestions

Pay Yourself First! Pay Yourself First! Pay Yourself First!

Many times, we have the truest intentions of putting money into a savings account. After paying bills, renting a couple of movies, ordering a pizza, dining out or entertainment, how much money do we have left to put into savings? A whopping zero—or close to it. Treat yourself as the most important bill you have and set aside 10% of your net income (take-home pay) and have it directly deposited into your savings account. The average American has less than two weeks worth of income in savings or checking. What would happen in case of a job loss, unexpected emergency, temporary lay-off, illness or accident? When you accumulate savings and encounter an unexpected emergency, you do not have to push the panic button and deal with the stress and anxiety. The list of unexpected emergencies is endless.

They normally happen at the worst time. We have all been there, even though we imagine it will never happen to us. Paying yourself first is one of the most important things you should do. Treat yourself as the most important bill you have. **Pay Yourself First!** Arrange to have a specific amount directly deducted from your paycheck. Set a goal to make this at least 10% of your gross income. Of course, you do have another option available to you: Work the rest of your life! Back to choices again. When you do many of the things I discuss, you will have your heart and brain going in two different directions.

Entertainment Fund and other expenditures

Entertainment is an area where many individuals overspend. Constantly dining out is usually the biggest expense for most consumers. Determine how much money you need each week or month and put it into your entertainment fund. The amount you decide on will help keep you from overspending. Take your lunch to work everyday. You will be very surprised how much this will save you. It could be hundreds of dollars each month! Consider using the envelope system—label different envelopes for different expenditures, for example, property taxes, car maintenance, and insurance companies that require a quarterly or annual payment. By making a thorough and complete budget, you can determine how much you need to set aside in each envelope. Then, when the bill is due in full, you will have saved enough in the envelope to cover the bill, instead of being blindsided by a bill you overlooked or were not prepared to pay. This also alleviates the possible use of a credit card, borrowing money, or getting a payday loan. Payday loans can charge 30%-575% interest. Yes, you read that correctly...30%-575%! Do everything you can to avoid payday loans. This financial pit will overwhelm you with interest fees alone. One last thing, no dipping into any envelopes for anything other than what it was intended for! Sorry, I never said this would be easy.

Retirement Fund

There are several different types of funds and investment vehicles available for planning your retirement. Company-sponsored retirement funds, such as 401(k) or 403(b), are some of the best benefits your employer can offer for your financial future, lifestyle, and peace of mind. Many companies match your contribution to a certain dollar amount or percentage. If the contribution is "before tax dollars," you are not only saving on taxes, you are earning an immediate return on your contribution. If you feel that you cannot afford to participate in your company-sponsored retirement plan, realize that contributing just 3% in before-tax dollars will have little or no effect in reducing your current net income (take-home pay). So, there is no excuse. There are several other investment vehicles to choose from, such as annuities (insurance), tax-deductible IRAs, and Roth IRAs. Seek a licensed advisor or broker to help with your investment decisions. **Please do not rely solely on Social Security**—it might not be enough for your needs. Do you know anyone who is living on their own and on Social Security, and is making ends meet? Most are not. Out of 100 individuals who retire, only 1-3 are self-sufficient! Take a minute and think of someone who is making ends meet with Social Security, alone.

When saving for retirement, time is not on your side if you don't act now, because of the magic of compounding interest. Here is a perfect example. Let's assume that you are 25 years old and you save $50 each month until you are age 65. Assume an average rate of return (15%) over the 40-year period. (Of course, there will be years when you will earn less and years when you will earn more over the 40-year time span.) At age 65, you will have $1,067,454. Quite impressive! Suppose you decide to start investing at age 35, a 10-year difference, which means you did not invest $6,000 ($50 x 12 months = $600 x 10 years = $6,000). Now how much will you have accumulated at age 65? $260,847! Waiting ten years and not investing the $6,000 will cost you and your family $806,607. Amazing! Contributing to a retirement program should be a top priority in your financial plan. Saving any amount is good. A little bit here, a little bit there. It all adds up! Write down your financial goals and gather any and all financial documents to get a realistic, specific plan in the works. Your goals may change from time to time. Review them often and do not hesitate to make adjustments when it is necessary.

Summary Questions For Chapter 1

The more money you make, the more you have?
A. True
B. False

The three types of goals are?
A. Long term
B. Budgeting
C. Short term
D. Mid term

Which statement is incorrect?
A. Write down your goals.
B. Believe in yourself that you will accomplish the goal.
C. Once you write down your goals, do not change them.
D. Review your goals after three months.

A _____ is a financial statement of estimated income and expenses.
A. Goal
B. Dream
C. Budget
D. Commitment

Which tool for budgeting is not correct?
A. Credit card statements
B. Pay stubs
C. Memory
D. Write down every penny you spend.

Which is most effective for a successful budget?
A. Credit card statements
B. Pay stubs
C. Memory
D. Write down every penny you spend.

When should I start these strategies?
A. Beginning of the month
B. End of the month
C. Pay day
D. Today

Non-essential expenditures are cable T.V, fast food, DVD player.
A. True
B. False

Name four essential expenditures.

A. _____

B. _____

C. _____

D. _____

Name two top sources of debt.

A. _____

B. _____

_____ of all spending is unplanned.

A. 50%
B. 65%
C. 35%
D. 41%

The number one reason people do not have an adequate retirement fund.

A. Spend too much on our children and grandchildren
B. Too much debt
C. We live day-to-day
D. Children's education

What should you pay first?

A. Mortgage
B. Credit card bills
C. Cable T.V
D. Yourself

According to The American Bar Association, _____ of all divorces are directly related to personal finances.

A. 23%
B. 50%
C. 89%
D. 37%

Contributing 3% of before-tax dollars into an employer-sponsored retirement plan will have little effect on your take home pay.

A. True
B. False

Chapter 2—Credit Cards, Paper or Plastic?

Chapter two discusses several aspects of credit cards—the different types, how to qualify for a credit card, how many and what kind you should have. We will also examine "nuisance fees" that lenders can add to your account balance and are normally imposed as a form of payment penalty.

Credit Cards

Credit cards (e.g., MasterCard, Visa, Discover) are issued by banks, savings and loans, and credit unions. The credit limit and interest rates are based on a consumer's credit history and many other factors that we will discuss later. Credit limits can vary considerably—from a few hundred dollars to thousands of dollars. Some banks are quite lenient with credit—the more they lend, the more interest they might charge. Other banks extend credit conservatively. Banks consider several factors when establishing a credit limit; most important is the consumer's credit rating. **Be wary of receiving credit limits that go beyond your ability to make the payments.** Credit cards yield high dividends for the issuer, accounting for as much as **75%** of all the profits earned annually by banks. You can now see why 2.5 billion credit card solicitations are mailed each year. Credit card companies also profit from charging merchants and service providers a fee (1%-4%) each time a customer uses that company's credit card in the merchant's establishment.

Note: As much as you would like to help your children, PLEASE do not either give them a credit card or allow access to yours as a co-user. You may be asking for trouble. We have seen so many instances of children maxing out their parents' credit cards. No matter whom you allow to use your credit card, YOU are responsible for paying the debt, and your credit report will be affected. Think twice before lending a credit card to family or friends.

Co-signing a credit card application or any loan should carefully be evaluated and discussed openly between all parties involved, using written, mandatory re-payment expectations. Who is responsible when the scheduled payment is not received on time? Both co-signers are responsible for on-time payments, so late payments are reported on both credit reports. A needless risk? It is your credit at stake. To be on the safe side, avoid co-signing for anyone. ANYONE.

There are several other types of credit cards in use today: Department store or merchant cards, travel and entertainment cards, gas/oil company credit cards, secured credit cards, reward, as well as ATM-Debit Cards. Let's review each type.

Department Store, Gas/Oil Company, Airline and Reward Cards

These types of credit cards seldom charge annual fees and encourage extended payments, both to spur buying and to earn interest for themselves, which, in many cases, can be quite high. The customer can also receive rewards—flight miles, a percentage donated to their university, etc.

Travel and Entertainment Cards

American Express, Diner's Club, Carte Blanche are not limited to travel and entertainment purposes at all. Many consumer items and services may be obtained with these cards. Cardholders may be charged a fee (conveniently referred to as membership fees) of $50-$300/year in some cases, and are usually required to pay the balances in full each month. Lenders who issue these cards are less tolerant of late payments and are quick to revoke privileges during a consumer's financial set back.

Secured Credit Cards

Secured credit cards require you to pay a deposit, normally $250-$1,000, which is held as collateral in a savings or CD account at the bank that is issuing the card. The amount deposited is your credit limit, sometimes a bit more. The secured credit card is normally issued to someone who is establishing credit or has some bumps and bruises on their credit report, such as late payments, collection accounts, home foreclosure, repossession, or other negative entries. Once your money has been deposited, you cannot withdraw any of the funds (principal or interest earned) without canceling your account. Some companies will convert the card, in time, to an unsecured card and then refund the security deposit plus interest.

ATM and Debit Cards

ATM and debit cards are issued by banks for use at automated teller machines and most businesses. Originally designed only as a method of withdrawing cash, they now perform many banking functions, including deposits, account inquiries, bank transfers, and even bill payments. If you have a line of credit with your bank, you can also draw on cash advances. When paying with one of these cards, the amount of your store purchase is automatically deducted from your checking or savings account. **Do not forget to immediately deduct your purchase amount from your checking or savings account balance.** When a card is lost and is used by someone else, that person can wipe out your entire balance. (There is no liability limit to the cardholder as there is with credit cards.)

Costs And Nuisance Fees Associated With Credit Cards

Interest Charges (APR)

Finance charges are based on the lender's Annual Percentage Rate (APR), which is the rate of interest charged by a creditor on an annual basis. Your card may have a "fixed" interest rate or a variable rate. In a variable rate program, changes in the rate raise or lower the finance charge on your account. "Fixed" rates are not locked in; the rate could be changed with a prior 15-day notification of the change from the issuer. The interest rate is only one way the credit card company makes money. You should use cards only with a low APR. A better idea— avoid using any credit cards. The exception would be using cards as a convenient way to pay—when the balance is paid in full every 1-2 months.

Late Fees

Most banks assess fees for late payments, which can be quite expensive. The fee could be $29-$35. Another penalty the bank can impose is to substantially increase your interest rate, even when you are only one day late. Look for credit cards that offer a grace period, which is the amount of time you have to pay off the balance without incurring any interest charges. Beware of cards that offer low rates and no annual fee. Many of these issuers do not offer grace periods and sometimes send statements out late intentionally to increase the probability of a late payment fee and a possible excuse for a substantial increase in the interest rate. Remember, if it sounds too good to be true, then it probably is. **Always read the fine print.** If the offer is too confusing and is not clear to you, it would be a good idea to refrain from applying for that particular credit card. Last year banks made **24 billion dollars** in late fees! **$24,000,000,000.**

Over-The-Limit-Fees

Credit card companies can charge you a penalty, called an over-the-limit-fee should you go over your credit limit and charge more than you actually have available to spend. Charges made beyond your credit limit are possible and allowed by many credit card issuers, whether you do it intentionally or it results from a bookkeeping error on your part. The fee charged by the bank will normally range from $29 to $35. When this happens, the bank will charge you the penalty plus the minimum amount due on your account. If the minimum payment due is $60, and the over-the-limit fee is $35, your total minimum payment due, in order to avoid ANOTHER over the limit fee and get back to a "current status" will be $95. This is like throwing money right out the window.

Annual Fees

These fees, sometimes referred to as membership fees, can range from $75 and higher. Contact the issuer to negotiate the removal of this fee. You will be surprised how many issuers will eliminate the annual fee just by asking, especially if you have been a long time client and have an excellent payment history. What is the worst thing they can say? No. When calling to negotiate a reduction in your interest rate, ask for a supervisor and politely ask whether they would consider lowering your interest rate. Your payment history must be very good before they will consider a reduction.

Transaction Fees

Anytime you request a change to your account, whether it is to change your due date, ask to lower your interest rate, and even when making your payment by phone, some credit issuers will add a transaction fee. Before making a change or payment by phone, ask if there are any fees associated with your transaction. Some credit card companies may even charge a minimum each time you use the card, normally 10 to 15 cents each time.

Pay-Off Fees

Almost everyone knows credit issuers make money from assessing and collecting interest. Many consumers pay their balance each month to avoid interest charges. Some banks actually penalize their customers for paying the monthly balance! A fee of $10-$15 may be charged to your account each month. More and more credit card issuers are doing this. Carefully review your monthly statements.

Cash Advances

Using your credit card for cash advances makes a very expensive loan. The interest rate charged on a cash advance could be as high as 24.9%-29.9%. A few issuers will charge a little less than that. Try to avoid cash advances unless you plan to pay the entire balance before they assess any interest charges. On some types of loans, the interest on the balance accrues every day. Call the card issuer and find out how your interest is calculated. Loans with interest accruing daily should be paid off as soon as possible.

Note: Let's say you take advantage of a credit card offering to do balance transfers at 0% interest with a $5,000 credit limit. Suppose you transfer $2,000 from a different account onto the new 0% credit card. You decide to go shopping and put $650 on the new card. Later, you decide to get a cash advance of $1,000 using the same account. The result:

- **$2,000 balance transfer at 0% interest**

- **$650 purchases at 7.9% interest**

- **$1,000 cash advance at 21.99%**

When you make a payment of $200, can you guess which of the three transactions the payment will be applied to? Usually the $200 payment will be applied to the balance transfer at 0%. All other monthly payments will also be applied to the 0% total until the balance transfer of $2,000 is paid in full. Then, any subsequent monthly payments will be applied to the purchases of $650 at 7.9%. Once that is paid in full, your monthly payments will be applied to the cash advance of $1,000 at 21.99%. Why does it work that way? Credit issuers make most of their revenue from interest charges. Your monthly payments will be applied to the lowest interest charge, then the second lowest interest charge, and so on. Is the interest continuing to accumulate on the unpaid balances at the higher rates? Call your credit card company and ask. The member services number is on the back of your card.

Items To Watch For On Your Credit Card Statement

Many consumers assume the information on their credit card statement is correct. That could be a costly assumption, especially since identity theft is the fastest growing crime in America, according to The Federal Bureau of Investigation. California ranks first in cases of identity theft, and Florida ranks fifth. Credit issuers can also make mistakes that could affect your statement. Let's take a look at the items on your credit card statement that should be reviewed every month. This will take you only a few minutes and is well worth the time spent. Do not allow any of those unexpected surprises. I like surprises, but the unexpected ones always seem to cost me a lot of money.

Previous Balance

The previous balance will show the total balance accumulated (amount you owe) before your payment has been applied. The previous balance should match last month's balance after a payment has been made to your account. Your current balance should be less than your previous balance, unless you are paying less than the minimum amount due. If you have a very high-interest credit card, even paying the minimum may not reduce your balance because your minimum payment is only enough to pay the interest charges. Beware that making only the minimum payment on a high-interest credit card may actually increase your balance. The minimum payment normally will not even cover the cost of interest charges. Your minimum monthly payment may be $189 per month, but your interest charges are $217 per month. This scenario is not unusual and could prevent you from ever paying the account in full. Please check your balances and rates. This is time well spent!

Payments and Credits

You should ALWAYS examine whether your last payment was applied correctly to your balance. Lenders do make mistakes. Please do not assume anything. We all know what happens when you assume. Review your statement carefully each month. It is your money. You earned it; you keep it.

Credits are posted after you have returned something back to a vendor; your account will be credited with the amount you were refunded. Please do not take for granted that your credited amount is correct. I have personally had three different charges on my accounts that I did not authorize. Thoroughly examining my statement, I saved almost $200 in unauthorized charges. $200 is $200. That is a lot of money to me! It doesn't make me a millionaire, but it does get me $200 closer. See "Charges" below.

Charges

Charges will show up as a result of any purchases you made with your credit card. Please check this EVERY month—sometimes vendors accidentally charge you for the same item or service twice. You may also find an item on your statement that you did not authorize or purchase. Keep in mind—identity theft is very easy to accomplish. Millions of consumers had their identities stolen in 2004. Every day, I talk to individuals who are victims of identity theft, and they never thought they would be. DO NOT ASSUME, especially when it comes to the money you have worked so hard for. Do not allow someone else to care more about YOUR money than you do!

Cash Advances

This is a very expensive loan, unless you plan on paying the entire balance and have a "grace period" before interest starts to accrue. Card issuers charge a hefty interest rate to give someone a cash advance. You will also need your personal PIN, supplied by the credit card company, in order for you to borrow any money. The bank requires the PIN in order to lend the consumer any money from their credit card. If you are requesting several cash advances, you might ask yourself whether you are living beyond your means, because this is a good indication that you might need some financial counseling. It is an option you may want to pursue and it only makes sense that you do the best you can do. Knowing your financial situation, and knowing the importance of budgeting and being able to account for all your monies is 100% less painful than retiring broke.

Finance Charges

Credit card companies can legally increase the interest rate charged to you with a written statement notifying you of the change (normally an increase) fifteen days prior to implementing it. Many credit issuers fill their billing statements with offers, such as magazines, rewards, and so on. Make sure you go through all the materials in your credit card statement. This will help avoid any unexpected surprises. This applies to more than just this paragraph, but ALWAYS read the fine print. Some consumers do not even read the big print.

Minimum Payment

This is the least amount the credit card company requires you to pay on the account. The minimum is normally 1 1/2% to 4% of the outstanding balance. Making only the minimum payment will take you several years to pay off the balance, assuming you do not add additional charges. Credit issuers really appreciate it when the minimum amount is paid. Why? One of the many ways card issuers earn money, as explained earlier, is by assessing INTEREST charges. Always pay more than the minimum amount due when possible. You keep the money (interest charges) in your pocket instead of putting it in their pocket.

Examples:
$1,000 balance at 2% is $20. $2,000 balance at 3% is $60. The $20 or the $60 would be your bare minimum payment.

Due Date

The due date is the date when the payment is due. It is important that you do not wait until the last minute to pay the bill. Send your payment at least ten days prior to the due date. Doing so will avoid your being charged any late fees because the issuer did not credit your payment on time. If you pay your bill online, it may still take several days for the payment to be credited to your account. Should you wait until the last minute and need to pay by phone to pay on time, you may be charged a fee from $10 to $14.95. Try to get into a financial position where you can pay any bills the same day they are received. That would be a great goal to strive for.

Credit Limit

The credit limit is the maximum amount of credit that you can spend on the credit card. Be careful that you do not have too much available credit, which can negatively impact your credit score (FICO or Beacon). You may be considered a high risk and be charged a higher interest rate, a longer payment period or both. Close accounts you are not using. Should you choose to close an account(s), please keep in mind the length of time you have had the card. Try to keep the cards you have had the longest time. The length of time you have had a credit card shows good payment history over a long period. Another great goal! Get rid of some of those credit cards. You are about to find out why.

What Is The Correct Number Of Credit Cards You Should Have?

The industry consensus is that a consumer should carry no more than five—a MasterCard, a VISA, a gas card, a department store card, and an ATM bank/debit card. Having anymore than that may work against you. Owning two to three would be better. Having these does not mean you have to use them. Use the privilege of having a credit card with responsibility. Having too much available credit could trigger to a potential lender that you do not have cash and are excessively depending on your cards.

Let's assume you have ten credit cards with a limit of $3,000 on each card, but you never carry any balances because you pay them in full each month. That is admirable and responsible, but do you know what the potential lender sees? Thirty thousand dollars of available unsecured credit! Let's assume you are downsized, sick, disabled, or are involved in a serious accident and cannot work. You can get money only from so many places, and let's assume that your credit cards are the only source of funds you have. It will not take long to max out $30,000 of available credit by paying the mortgage, groceries, utilities and all other essentials. Should that happen, potential lenders are going to evaluate your risk. Lenders take a close look at your potential debt. Having too much available credit will also affect your FICO and Beacon score, which we will discuss later. Closing accounts will not help your credit score, but if you have credit cards you do not use anymore or may have forgotten about, contact the credit issuer and ask that the account or accounts be closed. Ask them to send you verification that the account was **closed by the consumer**. Keep the oldest accounts as they show your long-time payment history, which is important when applying for a loan. A consumer with a credit card they have had for 10 years has a better tracking record than someone who has had a credit card for one or two years. Of course, a good payment history is also essential.

Limit Your Available Credit

Banks and credit issuers may increase your credit limit even if you did not request the increase. Do not think the issuer is rewarding you or indicating that you have the ability to pay for larger purchases. A high credit limit translates into higher interest payments. Should you receive a higher credit limit, consider contacting the issuer and asking them to lower it to the original amount of available credit. Remember, having too much available credit can hurt more than it helps when trying to secure a loan or lower interest rate.

Minimum Payments Do Not Add Up

Many consumers get locked into the idea that if they can make their minimum monthly payments, their credit cards will remain manageable. If the consumer is making additional purchases each month and making only the minimum payment, the debt will NEVER go down and continue to increase. This, in turn, increases the finance charges, which accrue and are based on the total balance. Lenders love consumers who make minimum payments. Please review the example below. Have you ever examined your credit card balance after making the minimum payment? The total balance due has barely gone down and should you have an account with high interest charges your balances may even GO UP!

Example: a credit card balance of $3,000 with an interest rate of 18%, and you pay the minimum payment of $60. To pay off the $3,000 balance will take approximately 451 months (37 years) and you will have paid $7,930.60 in interest. Wow! Wouldn't you rather have that $7,930.60 to use in ways that would benefit you and not them? Imagine what YOU could do with the money rather than giving it to a credit card company.

What would happen if you could add an additional $40 to the minimum payment of $60 for a total payment of $100? Now the $3,000 balance will be paid in 41 months (3 1/2 years) and you will have paid only $1,015.49 in interest. This is a very big difference—$6,951 to be exact. In summary, by adding an additional $40 to the original $60 payment over 3 1/2 years ($1,640) you saved almost $7,000 and reduced the time it would have taken to pay the balance by 402 months. Always try to pay more than the minimum payment, even if it is only $5-$10 per month. Every little bit will make a difference. Another goal!

Check Cashing Companies, Title for Loan, "Buy Here/Pay Here"

My recommendation regarding these companies in two words—avoid them! Interest rates at these establishments can be 157%-300%. Falling into this so-called "help and solution service" will cost you dearly. Paying back this type of debt can get out of control very quickly. Reading their fine print might discourage you from wanting to dig yourself a very big hole. Being in a position where you rely on these organizations may be an indication that you need professional counseling. Do not think you are alone—far from it. Professional help can make all the difference. I, myself, sought professional counseling regarding my personal finances. My wife has 10 months to finish her debt management program. Forget about pride, ego, and anything else that would cause you not to ask for help. I don't understand what is wrong with asking for help when it is available. We have all probably asked for help sometime in our lives, more than once, I am sure. Someday, someone may ask you for help or already has. If you could, wouldn't you jump at the chance to change someone's life, even if for one second?

Roll-Up Process

This is the quickest way to pay and eliminate your debt. Arrange your credit cards by interest rate, highest to lowest. Once you have paid-off the highest-rate credit card, like in the example above, take the extra $100 ($60 plus $40) you now have and apply it along with the minimum payment due on your second credit card. Assuming the same scenario as above, now you have $160 being applied to the balance of the second credit card. After the second credit card is paid in full, take the $160 and the minimum payment on the third credit card and now you have $220 being applied to the balance of the third credit card. Continue this process and you should be completely out of credit card debt in about 3-5 years or sooner depending on your credit card balances. Now you can use the money you were paying on credit cards for something else, like your retirement fund, an IRA, down payment for a house, a child's college education, an emergency fund, and so on. If you are paying more than the minimum payment on each of your cards, this roll up process will work much better and faster.

The Four Basic Types Of Credit Transactions

1. Secured Credit

Secured credit is any purchase backed by collateral. Some item of equal or greater value than the amount of the loan is pledged to the lender, so that failure to repay the loan results in the lender possessing the item as collateral. Collateral used for the advanced loan may be a car, jewelry, your home or real estate, or any other tangible asset that the client and lender agree to. The collateral provides the lender the least amount of risk, because if you fail to make your payments, the lender will keep or take the collateral. This is the easiest type of loan to obtain.

2. Unsecured Credit Cards

Unsecured credit is established when a lender extends credit to a client based upon their ability to pay. No collateral is required, but a finance charge is calculated against the total outstanding balance in order to encourage the client to maintain timely payments. Because there is no collateral with this type of credit, the lender has a much higher risk and, therefore, must have confidence in a client's ability to pay. Qualifying for unsecured credit is based on a variety of factors, such as the client's credit history, current financial status, employment, debt-to-income ratio, FICO score, and so on. In case the client defaults, the lender must go to court in order to seize assets and recover funds. Wage garnishment is a good example.

3. Installment Credit

Installment credit can be either secured or unsecured. Clients are granted a loan or credit, which must be repaid over a specific time period. Common installment loans are mortgages, automobile loans, personal loans and educational loans. If you fail to make timely payments, you are charged a late fee, and it will be reported to the credit reporting agencies as a negative entry.

4. Non-Installment Credit

Any bill that says "payment due upon receipt of this bill." Your telephone, utility, cable and a physician's statement are all common examples of non-installment credit.

Types Of Interest Loans

Simple Interest Loan

Simple interest is the best of the three. A simple interest loan allows you to make additional payments on your loan to reduce the principal (amount financed), which, in turn, allows you to pay the loan faster without penalty. Another benefit is saving on interest charges. Credit cards, your mortgage, a typical car loan are examples of simple interest loan agreements. Always ask the lender for a simple interest loan. Lenders are required by law to disclose that information to you. It should also be stated in the contract, but sometimes the wording is confusing or you might not read all the fine print.

Rule-Of-78 Loan

With a Rule-of-78 loan, most, if not your entire payment for months or even years (depending on the amount of time you financed the loan) is applied to interest only. For a time, none of the payment made on the account is applied to the principal (amount financed). Making extra payments on this type of loan does not reduce your principal or the next month's payment. In other words, although you might assume that making an additional $50 payment would reduce your next month's payment by $50, this would not be true. If your normal payment is $200 and you make that additional payment of $50, your next month's payment will still be $200—not $150. This type of loan can also penalize you for making extra or additional principal payments.

Add-On Interest Loan

This is the worst and is normally offered at "buy here pay here" establishments. Buy a car from a dealer that offers the "add-on interest calculation" and the car costs $20,000 at an interest rate of 20%. This is how it works: $20,000 x 20% is $4,000. The $4,000 is added to the purchase price of $20,000.00, which equals $24,000. You are charged interest on that amount, $24,000, instead of $20,000. You are literally being charged interest on interest. What a deal...for the vendor!

Reasons Why You Might Be Denied Credit

• Delinquent credit obligations, making late payments, outstanding debts, too much available credit, collection accounts, charge-offs, repossessions, foreclosures, filing bankruptcy—all mark you as being a risky customer. You can fix that!

• An incomplete credit application, such as omitting important information on a credit application, or discrepancies between the application and the credit file will suggest to the potential lender that a consumer is hiding information.

• Too many inquiries on a credit report give lenders the impression that you are desperately trying to obtain credit everywhere or have been rejected elsewhere. Limit credit inquiries to no more than two every six months. Credit inquiries stay on your credit report for two years. Each inquiry may reduce your FICO score by 5-9 points. (FICO score to be discussed later.) This DOES NOT include inquiries you make to check the accuracy of your credit report or inquiries from lenders who look at your credit history to possibly offer you an account. Your current lenders may also review your credit from time to time, which does not affect your FICO score.

• Errors in a file may simply arise from clerical mistakes, such as confusing customers with similar names, incorrect Social Security numbers, a recent address change, incorrect information reported by a lender. All can create problems. A credit bureau handles over 200 million files, so the possibility for error is tremendous. Seventy-five percent of all credit reports have some type of error on them. It is necessary to review reports from all three of the credit reporting agencies at least once per year, preferably every six months. That is the only way your files can be kept correct and up-to-date, and by taking the necessary steps to correct errors. **MAKE THIS A DEFINITE GOAL!**

❖ Insufficient credit files, meaning you have not been able to create or accumulate enough credit information in order for the lender to make an informed decision, based on your credit history.

❖ No credit history, which will not allow a potential lender to evaluate your payment history. You may be viewed as a bad credit risk to the lender when there is little or no credit history.

❖ Too young. You must be at least 18 years of age in order to get a credit card. (I believe the age should be raised to 24.) Two most difficult things our college men and women deal with are student loans and credit card debt. Some banks set up shop at a college to sign up more members. 99.99 % of the new members are college students. When your daughter or son gets the first credit card, explain to them exactly how it works. Credit cards should be used wisely. Maxing out your credit card on pizza, dates, beverages, tuition, books, or the next mechanical gadget can happen in the blink of an eye.

Prevent Credit Card Debt

It is clear that owning and using a credit card is a powerful and often expensive **privilege** for today's consumer. It is easy to have empathy for anyone who unwittingly creates a serious debt situation. We are only human and EVERYONE wants your money. Sadly, we give it to them most of the time. The combination of the ability to charge on impulse, bombardment from advertisers selling their products and services, along with confusing billing policies of banks, can result in seemingly insurmountable debt. For the first time ever, consumer debt has reached **1.5 trillion dollars.** It is difficult to fathom that number, but it breaks down to each and every family having over $8,000 in debt. Before using your credit card, consider these steps to avoid the possibility of having unmanageable credit card debt. Credit card debt has a way of sneaking up on you.

Many Americans are going overboard with the use of credit cards. Instead:

1. Use cash only. $$$$$$ Paper, NOT plastic!

2. Avoid accumulating any additional debt—any debt—not just credit card debt.

3. Limit the number of cards you have, especially if you rarely or never use them anymore.

4. Do not maintain credit cards with high interest rates. Negotiate a lower rate!

5. Limit your available credit. Having too much available credit may hurt you.

6. Always pay more than the minimum and use the roll-up process. Pay whatever you can afford.

7. Avoid credit cards with complicated billing policies.

8. Leave your credit cards at home in a safe place. We always spend more when our credit cards are easily available.

9. Tell yourself "**no**" more often. You may only think you need to buy the item!

10. Are you buying something essential or non-essential? Must you have it, or do you just want it?

11. Wait 3-5 days before making a big purchase; avoid buyer's remorse.

12. Avoid impulse buying. **Remember: 65% of the purchases we make are unplanned.**

13. Take someone with you to help control your spending.

14. Make a list of things you need, approximate the cost, take cash and stick to the list.

15. Have a specific plan (goals) **WRITE THEM DOWN!** This is your pathway to the better financial place.

16. I never said this would be easy. The reward is one hundred-fold greater than the effort!

Summary Questions For Chapter 2

Name three types of credit cards.
A. _____
B. _____
C. _____

Over-the-limit fees are assessed when you exceed your credit limit.
A. True
B. False

Secured credit cards require that you pay a deposit.
A. True
B. False

How many credit card solicitations are mailed each year?
A. 1.5 million
B. 2.5 million
C. 2.5 billion
D. 1.5 billion

You can call your bank and negotiate a lower interest rate.
A. True
B. False

Credit cards are described as:
A. Add-on interest loans
B. Simple interest loans
C. Rule of 78 loans
D. APR

What is the correct number of credit cards you should have?
A. None
B. 3
C. 8
D. 5

Always make the minimum payment.
A. True
B. False

Having as many credit cards as possible will increase the chances of qualifying for a loan.
A. True
B. False

What is the quickest way to pay off your debt?
A. Taking out a loan to pay all balances
B. Cash advances
C. Borrowing the money from a family member or friend
D. The roll-up process

Unsecured debt is backed by collateral.
A. True
B. False

A car loan or mortgage loan is unsecured debt.
A. True
B. False

How often should you check your credit report from each agency for accuracy?
A. Every five years
B. Never; it is not your responsibility.
C. Twice a year or a minimum of once per year
D. Every two years

Each inquiry to your credit file may reduce your FICO score by 5-9 points.
A. True
B. False

Chapter 3—Debt-to-Income Ratio

Debt-to-Income-Ratio is used by lenders to determine whether, in their opinion, you are carrying a safe or excessive amount of debt. This is the most common way lenders calculate your ability to repay a loan. This ratio tells the lender the percentage of your net income that is being used to pay your debts. The debts used in the debt-to-income formula may include, but are not limited to, credit card payments, auto loans, student loans, bank loans, credit union loans, most secured loans and collection accounts. In order to determine your own debt-to-income ratio, calculate your net income, which includes employment net income, alimony payments, commissions, employer bonuses, tips, dividend interest, Social Security pensions and other government assistance. Let's assume your total monthly income is equal to $2,500 and your total monthly debt (excluding mortgage or rent) is $900. Divide the net monthly debt by your total monthly income.

$900 (debt) ÷ $2,500 (income) = 36%

Thirty six percent is your debt-to-income ratio. Is that good? In general, lenders view your ratio like this: 10%-20% is considered excellent to very good; 20% to 35% is considered questionable and will be looked at very closely, including possibly requiring that you provide proof of all income. At this stage, you should seriously consider increasing your income or decreasing your debt. The lender will examine your spending habits and where your money is being spent. If you are in this category, take a realistic look at a reputable, non-profit credit counseling/debt management/consolidation organization as a possible choice and as a potential solution. If your debt-to-income ratio is above 35%, seriously consider the help and professional services of a non-profit credit counseling/debt consolidation organization.

Not including mortgage or rent payments, your debt-to-income ratio goal should be at least 10%-20% . There are NO quick fixes to reducing expenses or increasing income. Continuing to monitor your ratio is very important for several reasons. You will be able to make good, sound financial decisions when applying for a loan, such as for a car, boat, home, child's education or recreational vehicle. You will also be able to avoid financial problems by knowing exactly where you stand financially, thus avoiding collections, garnishments, repossessions, legal action, foreclosure, or bankruptcy.

What Do You Mean By a Reputable Debt Management/ Credit Counseling Agency? How Can I Be Sure?

In today's society, savvy consumers know it is healthy and wise to be skeptical. Since 9-11, many people's lives have been changed financially and turned upside down for the worse. Many so-called "non-profit" organizations are nothing more than a scam to take your money. The best choice of words I can use to describe these companies is "unscrupulous businesses preying on people's fears and trust." Such companies are usually concerned with one thing—lining their own pockets with money from the individuals who entrusted them for help at a time when they needed it.

Before engaging their services, here are some questions you should ask such a potential firm, in order to be sure you are working with a company that is legitimate, caring, compassionate, qualified, properly regulated, and effective with creditors.

1. Is the company a legally recognized, non-profit organization by the Internal Revenue Service?

2. Do they provide on-going training for their counselors?

3. Are their counselors "Certified Counselors?" Certification requires several months of intensive classroom training, and passing a very thorough exam. Training for counselors should be ongoing and a continuous process.

4. Is the company ISO-Certified (International Standards Organization)? This is probably the strictest regulator in the industry, although certification is not required. Companies that are ISO-certified volunteered to complete the certification process. ISO can penalize certified companies tens of thousands of dollars for not adhering to proper business practices and ethics. Counselors are continually monitored by management, paperwork must be perfect, procedures followed strictly. Audits are conducted twice per year by the ISO to make sure all policies and procedures are strictly followed. All counselors must sign a Code of Ethics Agreement, which is not taken lightly by the debt management company or the ISO. The fee to be certified is also quite expensive.

5. Does the company offer education to help consumers who are dealing with financial challenges? If so, what kinds and how much?

6. Are clients' accounts insured?

7. Is the company licensed, bonded and insured?

8. What other regulatory agencies do you report to, such as the Internal Revenue Service, FTC (Federal Trade Commission), that state's Attorney General's Office and Banking Authority, NFCE, ISO.

Summary Questions For Chapter 3

The calculation of how much of your net income is being spent on bills is called:
A. Rule of 78
B. Income-to-debt ratio
C. Income goals
D. Debt-to-income ratio

Having a debt-to-income ratio of 40% is good?
A. True
B. False

Increasing debt is a perfect way to reduce your debt-to-income ratio.
A. True
B. False

Keeping track of your debt-to-income ratio could help you save money.
A. True
B. False

Chapter 4—Is Your Debt Getting Out Of Control?

It is important to recognize some of the warning signs of potential debt problems. Hoping that checks do not clear the bank before you are paid, not being able to pay your bills on time, borrowing from friends and family, applying for a pay-day loan, getting a cash advance to pay bills are a few of the warning signs. I believe the biggest sign is when you are able to admit to yourself that you are having financial challenges and need help. You may be living beyond your means, have experienced an unexpected emergency or many other circumstances over which you had no control. The most important thing is recognizing your situation before it gets out of control or becomes more difficult to manage. Sometimes we tend to wait until the last minute or are backed into a corner, something like having a toothache and taking an aspirin to temporarily stop the pain. Weeks later, you find yourself taking an aspirin every few hours to stop the pain. Finally, after several months you decide to see your dentist, because the aspirin is not working anymore. Bad news! Because you procrastinated and postponed the visit to the dentist, what would have been a $60 filling is now an $800 root canal job, or worse, the tooth must be removed and replaced with a cap, for a thousand dollars or more.

Do not ignore your creditors when they call or send notices in the mail. I know that is sometimes easier said than done. Some collectors may be rude, threatening, and make you feel less than a person. Be the bigger person. Most creditors want to help you as much as possible, and many have temporary programs that may solve your financial challenge. Ignoring them will only make things worse and may eliminate any possibility that they will help in any way. When you call them, have a realistic payment plan in mind that you can afford each month. Do not promise a payment you know you cannot make. When you are unrealistic about what you can pay or don't make payments as agreed, they may put a stop to any programs or help they can offer. Ask if they will postpone your payments for a specific period of time, maybe two or three months. They may be able to make a deferment, that is, put the current payment on the end of a loan. This typically works better for secured debt, such as a car and even your home. Here is how it works.

Let's assume your car note will be paid off in March 2006, but you do not have the funds to pay the current amount due. The collector agrees to defer one month, which means they will take the current monthly amount due and put it on the end of the loan. Now your car note will be paid off in April 2006, one month later than the original pay-off date. Even though many creditors are rude, please be polite and respectful—yes sir, no sir, please and thank you. Most collectors will go out of their way to help you. Many consumers are just as rude or worse, calling the collector every name in the book. How would you feel after listening to that all day? Some consumers' excuses for not making timely payments are ridiculous. The truth is always the best but not the easiest action to take with your creditors. Always treat people the way you would like to be treated. You will be surprised how many doors that approach opens for you. You always get more with sugar than vinegar!

Call your credit card company and see whether you can negotiate the interest rate you are paying. Contact customer service at the telephone number on the back of your card. Normally, the person who answers your call is not in the position to lower your rate. Sometimes you must explain why you are calling and he/she will transfer you to a supervisor. Let them know you are getting solicitations on a daily basis from other credit card companies, and the rates being offered are much lower than the rate you are currently paying. As long as you have been making your payments on time, most companies will reduce your rate. The reduction in your rate is usually temporary. The lower negotiated rate is normally in effect for 3-6 months. Sometimes the new rate will be permanent if you have been doing business with them for a long time. Again, you must have a good payment history. Now, what is the worst that could happen? They say no. Let me give you an example of what lowering your interest rate can do for you.

Let's say you have a $1,000 balance at a rate of 22%. It will take you 11 years to pay off that balance by making the minimum payment, 9 years at 20%, 8 years at 18%, 7 years at 16%, and 6 years at 14%. You will also save plenty on interest charges. Please do not hesitate to wheel and deal. Companies do not want to lose your business.

What do you do when none of these methods works? Now what? Contact a reputable, non-profit credit counseling/debt management organization. These types of agencies have a pre-arranged agreement with most creditors for putting together a repayment plan that is affordable for you and satisfies the issuer. Take the weight off your shoulders and place it on theirs. That is why they are there—to provide help in the form of guidance, motivation, education and anything else within their guidelines. And you will not be judged! Credit counseling agencies work very hard to lower your interest rates (so the debt is paid in a shorter period of time), lower the payment (to increase your monthly cash flow), eliminate late fees and over the limit fees, and re-age your accounts (so that you can start with a clean slate). Please do not misunderstand. This is not a quick fix, but after a year or so, you will have a much better chance to qualify for credit.

I do not want to contradict something I said earlier, namely, do not accumulate any additional debt. The purpose of obtaining all the benefits and services provided by a credit counseling/debt management organization is to **GET YOURSELF OUT OF DEBT.** Your monthly debt payments may be reduced from 20% to 40% depending on the creditors, since they all have different policies and procedures. Some will reduce the interest rate and possibly eliminate it altogether, or reduce your monthly payment, sometimes both or neither. Again, it all depends on your creditors. Credit counseling agencies have helped millions of families for a long time. **YOU ARE NOT ALONE.** Do not overlook or dismiss this option to help get yourself back on track with your finances. This is not a handout or charity. They use YOUR money to pay the debt. Enrolling in a credit counseling company's debt management program is extremely effective and will eliminate all the negative aspects of being in over your head with debt. Get rid of the stress. Enrolling in a credit counseling program is 100% confidential. No one will ever know unless you tell someone.

Okay, you say, I've tried all those things and creditors are still harassing me, both at work and home. What should I do? Getting a harassing call from a creditor can definitely put a damper on your day and a chink in your neck, adding stress, anxiety, anger, and cause you to be less productive at work and less focused on what you should be doing. First, politely ask the collectors to stop calling you at work or home. If that doesn't work, send the collection department a civil request (by certified mail) to stop calling as you have asked in the past. This process is called "cease and desist" and is communicated to the lender by way of a letter, sent by certified mail, return receipt requested. Provide your name, account number, address, phone number (optional), and ask that they no longer contact you by phone, either at home or work. They will continue to contact you by mail; stopping the calling does not eliminate your debt obligations.

One of the unpleasant consequences of ignoring a creditor is being taken to court. The creditor will win the lawsuit nine out of ten times. Creditors understand that a court can be an intimidating place, so they file a lawsuit knowing that the consumer may not appear. If so, the attorney wins the case by default, and now has the ability to garnish your wages, up to 25% or more. They also have the right to take your property. The creditor has nothing to lose, and everything to gain by taking you to court. Avoid this situation by keeping in touch with your creditors. Please do not ignore them! Having your wages garnished could jeopardize your job and you know how quickly news travels around the office, which can be very embarrassing for you. Keep this anthill from becoming a mountain. Stay in contact with your creditors. Should your creditors not be able to work with you, seek professional services.

Charged-Off Accounts

When an account has been charged-off, the creditor has exhausted all methods of collection and simply gives up. Rather than taking legal action, the creditor reports the charge-off to all three credit-reporting agencies as a negative entry, which will remain a sore spot on your credit report for at least seven years. Even though the debt has been charged-off, you still owe the money. Just one charged-off account can keep you from obtaining any credit, like a car loan, credit card, mortgage or student loan, qualifying for an apartment and even qualifying for a job. A charged-off account will haunt you until the debt is paid. Getting credit when you have an account charged off is not impossible, but at the very least, you will pay higher fees, such as interest rate, because you are viewed as a poor credit risk. You could also be turned down for the loan you are applying for. We have clients paying 18%-25% on their automobile loans due to charge-offs. That it a pretty stiff penalty! Pay any charged-off accounts using a specific repayment plan. Keep your promise of paying what was agreed to by all parties. Intentions and promises are two completely different concepts.

Do I Have Any Options?

Yes. The bottom line is that the lenders want their money. Therefore, calculate an affordable amount you can pay each and every month until the debt is paid in full. Many lenders will settle for as little as 30%-60% of the total debt that is due. In this scenario, the lender normally wants the entire, negotiated amount paid in full, but might arrange a monthly payment plan. Even though you have shown you are willing to pay the amount and do, future lenders may still look at this negatively. Over time, the charged-off settlement will be viewed as a positive step on your part, but it will take awhile. Once you have paid the settled amount, send a copy of the arrangement to the credit reporting agencies, showing it paid in full, which may help turn the negative rating into a positive rating a little sooner.

Summary Questions For Chapter 4

Name two warning signs that show your debt may be getting out of control.

A. _____

B. _____

Ignore any communication with your creditors.

A. True

B. False

When you are contacted by a collector,

A. Hang up on them.

B. Do not answer the phone.

C. Deal with them politely and courteously.

D. Pretend you are not the party they are trying to reach.

Briefly explain the term "deferment."

_____

_____

_____

_____

When you simply cannot make your debt payments any longer, you should:

A. Give up.

B. File for bankruptcy.

C. Contact a non-profit credit counseling/debt management company.

D. Ignore them until your financial situation gets better.

The main purpose of a credit-counseling agency is to:

A. Get you out of debt

B. Stop harassing collection calls.

C. Work out an affordable payment for yourself and your family.

D. All the above

What can be the result if a creditor takes you to court (files a lawsuit) and wins?
A. Your wages can be garnished.
B. The attorney can have you fired from your job.
C. You will go to jail.
D. Leave the country.

When an account has been charged off, you no longer owe the money.
A. True
B. False

How long will a charged-off account remain on your credit report?
A. 2 years
B. 7 years
C. Forever
D. Until it is paid in full

Credit counseling agencies will help:
A. With your investments
B. Pay your debt for you
C. Prepare and initiate a repayment plan with the creditors you choose to put into the program
D. Give you legal advice

What is the most effective way to put a stop to harassing phone calls from collectors?

_____

_____

Chapter 5—I Cannot Pay My Debts

Unpaid Debts

Here is a brief description and examples of what could happen if you do not pay your debt, whether secured or unsecured.

If you hold a secured credit card (one that requires a deposit) and discontinue paying your monthly bill, the issuer will revoke your charging privileges, seize your deposit and, of course, report the situation to the credit reporting agencies as a negative entry.

If you fail to make your car payment and fall behind, the bank has the legal right to repossess your car without your permission. The car now belongs to the lender, who will most likely sell it at an auction. Let's assume you owe $10,000 on the car and it sells for $2,000 at the auction. Guess who is responsible for paying the $8,000 balance, towing charges, and any administrative costs? YOU! Now you must pay for something you no longer own and cannot use. Remember, at the first sight of potential problems in paying the car note, contact the lender to see whether you can come up with a mutual agreement. Believe it or not, the lender does not want to repossess the car. From this example, the lender also lost a lot of money. They are in business to make money, not lose it. Lenders are open to the idea of working something out with clients, a solution that will benefit both parties. Please do not bury your head in the sand and ignore the problem. You WILL lose!

After paying yourself first, ALWAYS pay your mortgage on time. We all need a roof over our head. Should you default on your mortgage payment, the lender has the right to foreclose (seize) the home and also keep all the equity that has accumulated. This is the most devastating loss you and your family can sustain. There are some steps you can take to avoid foreclosure, a homeowner's worst nightmare. Contact the lender and see whether you can negotiate a lower payment, which is usually temporary, but can also be a permanent solution. A typical workout plan, called " a cure," is adding a percentage of the outstanding debt to regular monthly payments until the debt becomes current. In this case, your mortgage payment will be higher until you become current in dealing with the amount formerly in arrears. Consider a part time job, a roommate, selling assets, readjusting your lifestyle, borrowing from a relative or friend. Sometimes, we have to do what we have to do. Keep in mind that these suggestions are only temporary until you get back on your feet.

Another option is deferring payments, as we discussed earlier. This option allows you to eliminate the current payment by deferring that amount to the end of the loan. In other words, if your mortgage would have been paid in full in January 2029, by deferring 3 months of current payments, the mortgage will be paid in April 2029. To explore all workable options, seek the advice of an attorney.

You have heard the saying that everything is negotiable. It is almost always in the best interest of the lender and debtor, alike, to try to maintain a mutually satisfactory arrangement through a feasible workout of some kind. The lender wants customers, not litigants. If all fails...SELL!

There are basically three different things that could happen when a consumer does not pay on department store credit cards, unsecured credit cards, medical bills, attorney fees, hospital bills—these kinds of bills. They are: cancellation of charging privileges, damage to your credit rating, a requirement to go to court and possibly have your wages garnished.

Not paying your credit card bills will result in the account being closed by the issuer, and all charging privileges will be terminated. The issuer will continue to attempt to collect the debt. If they are unable to, your account will eventually be turned over to a collection agency. This will be reflected on your credit report as a collection account. The resulting credit rating and credit score will have a negative impact on your ability to get a loan of any type.

Further, your credit will be severely damaged. Should you be contacted by a collection agency, they may tell you if they do not receive a payment, your credit will be ruined. Well, unfortunately your account is probably already 30, 60, 90, or 120 days past due and already shows on your credit report as a negative entry and that the account has been turned over to a collection agency. Therefore, your credit has already been damaged. This does not mean you should not try to work something out with the collector. Remember, you are still responsible to pay any monies owed.

When you fall behind on payments to a lender of an unsecured debt, the lender has the legal right to sue in order to get what is owed to them. Since property was not pledged as collateral, a court judgement is required in order for the lender either to seize property and/or exercise the option of garnishing your wages 25% or more. Often times, these threats are a scare tactic used to intimidate you into paying. Even so, I would not assume anything. The best solution is for both the lender and customer to negotiate some type of mutual settlement.

The Fair Credit Collection Practices Act (FDCPA)

What debt collectors cannot do:

1. Give misleading or false information about the debt to others.

2. Call after 9:00 p.m. or before 8:00 am within the client's time zone.

3. Interrupt the work routine of a client's employment.

4. Make excessive calls to clients at home or work as a method of harassment.

5. Send any letter that may look like an official government document.

6. Threaten a client or family member in a physical or illegal manner.

7. Imply that physical damage may occur to the client's property.

8. Deposit a post-dated check before the date on the check.

9. Misrepresent themselves as a government agency or a law practice.

10. Continue to harass a client after being notified in writing (certified mail) to cease and desist all contact by phone.

Collection agents have rights, but they also must adhere to specific responsibilities. Make sure they do not abuse your rights.

Bankruptcy—Seek The Advice of a Qualified Bankruptcy Attorney

Bankruptcy is a serious decision, but is a viable option. There are three types of bankruptcy, and we will be covering only Chapter 7 bankruptcy and Chapter 13 bankruptcy. There is also Chapter 11, which is designed to help corporations.

Chapter 7

Chapter 7 bankruptcy absolves the consumer from any debt filed under it. It allows an individual to discharge virtually all unsecured debt. The debtor loses all property, except that exempt by law. Some states allow the consumer to keep necessary items, such as a car and home. What you can keep varies from state to state, which is why you should seek the expertise of a bankruptcy attorney in your state. Fees can vary substantially. Do not hesitate to ask questions until you completely understand the benefits and consequences of filing bankruptcy. Once bankruptcy is discharged, the consumer will have no debt from anything filed under that specific bankruptcy. Chapter 7 may be filed once every 7 years but will remain on your credit reports for ten years.

Chapter 13

Chapter 13 bankruptcy is for individuals who wish to reorganize their debts and seek court protection while they plan a reorganization with creditors. Under this Chapter, the debtor arranges to pay back all or part of their debts over a period of 3 to 5 years. A Chapter 13 bankruptcy will also stay on your credit reports for 10 years. Unlike the Chapter 7 bankruptcy, a Chapter 13 bankruptcy can be filed during any difficult financial situation.

Bankruptcy should not be viewed as the end of financial success, but rather a turning point toward a wise financial future. Again, bankruptcy does not have to be the end of hopes and dreams but rather an opportunity to start over again! Never give up!

Summary Questions For Chapter 5

If I can't make the payments on my car and miss several,
A. the lender must call me before taking any action.
B. the lender must have my permission before repossessing the car.
C. the automobile will be repossessed without my consent or knowledge.
D. None of the above

After paying yourself first, always pay the _____ next.
A. Credit card bills
B. Cable T.V
C. Utilities
D. Mortgage

A $14,000, repossessed automobile is sold at auction for $6,000. Who pays the difference?
A. The dealer
B. The auctioneer
C. The bank or lender
D. The original owner

Because of the Fair Credit Collection Practices Act (FDCPA), collectors and creditors
A. can call any time.
B. can call only between 10:00 a.m. - 6:00 p.m.
C. must discontinue calling after receiving a cease and desist letter.
D. can come to your home and take something equal to the amount owed.

When considering bankruptcy, seek the advice of a credit-counseling agency.
A. True
B. False

The following bankruptcy stays on your credit report for ten years:
A. Chapter 7
B. Chapter 13
C. Both
D. Neither

Chapter 7 is a reorganization of your unsecured debt.
A. True
B. False

Bankruptcy is the end of your financial hopes and dreams.
A. Absolutely...throw in the towel
B. Not at all...never give up!

Chapter 6—Credit Reports and Credit Scoring

There are three major credit reporting agencies. It is very important that you review each credit report at least once per year, preferably every six months. Keep in mind that 3 out of 4 credit reports contain incorrect or outdated information. Before applying for a loan, be sure to check your credit report in order to avoid any unexpected surprises. In addition, keep in mind the rapid acceleration of identity theft, the fastest growing crime in America. Every day I talk to people who thought identity theft would never happen to them. Why take the risk? Obtain and review your credit reports—a great "short term goal."

The three major credit reporting agencies:

Experian National Consumer Assistance Center (formerly TRW)
P.O. Box 2104
Allen, TX 75013-2104
www.experian.com
(888) 397-3742

TransUnion Corporation
P.O. Box 390
Springfield, PA 19046-0390
www.transunion.com
(800) 888-4213

Equifax Credit Information Service
P.O. Box 740241
Atlanta, GA 30374
www.equifax.com
(800) 685-1111

Stop Receiving Credit Card Solicitations

You are familiar with the telemarketing "Do Not Call" list, and now you can also request not to receive credit card offers. The automated program is called **"The Opt Out Option,"** and the phone number is **(888) 567-8688**. There is no charge for this service and the process will take less than 5 minutes. You will be asked to choose between not receiving offers for 2 years or 10 years. Call NOW! Another short-term GOAL opportunity!

Together, these three credit reporting agencies maintain files on more than 200 million Americans and more than 12 million businesses. Each agency has the ability to track the credit history on any American, regardless of location. Each credit bureau will maintain different information on your credit history; what appears on one credit report may not appear on another. For this reason, it is very important that you receive a credit report from each agency.

Imagine looking at your Equifax report prior to applying for a car loan. It looks perfect, so you apply for the car loan with extreme confidence. What a surprise when you find out that the automobile dealership or lender uses Experian, and the information reported on the Equifax report does not match the other one. The Experian report shows derogatory information that is not shown on your perfect Equifax report. In order to get your most accurate credit history, order a copy from all three agencies. Not all creditors report to all three credit reporting agencies. The best way to make sure that the three reports are accurate is to order a "merged report," which shows information from the three agencies on one form.

Reading and Understanding Your Credit Report

The cover page should give a basic overview of the client's accurate name, Social Security number, and address. There may be a brief explanation on how the information was obtained and used, as well as the types of items affecting credit worthiness. Each of the three credit reporting agencies normally includes detailed instructions on how to read and understand the information on their report. Inside the report, any items that may show negatively will be marked with a minus. Examples are foreclosures, repossessions, judgements, liens, charge-offs, bankruptcies, and collections with each company filing the date posted. Specific account status will be listed for collection agencies, giving addresses, account numbers, current status, and the identification of the original lender. For each claim will be listed the date reported, terms of payment, responsible party, credit amount limit, recent balance, and comments on account history.

Your credit reports should list the same account information, giving favorable facts regarding sources and payment history. Each report will then list any requests received for the credit report, including those from the client. Many clients do not realize that applying for a loan will trigger a credit check by credit card issuers, banks, loan officers, and mortgage companies. When you apply for a new credit card or an increase on a current credit card, most creditors will require a credit check to assess the borrower's stability of employment and income.

Lastly, the report will disclose the client's personal information, including previous residences, possibly your driver's license number, telephone number, Social Security number, current and previous employers, date of birth, and spouse's name. I cannot stress enough the importance of making sure all the information is correct. Trying to repair or delete any incorrect information after the fact can be like climbing Mount Everest. Preventive medicine comes to mind. Again, DO NOT ASSUME ANYTHING! Credit reports can be accessed immediately through the Internet. Depending on what you order, just a credit report, a merged report, credit scores, and other services offered, the costs will vary. You will need to use a credit card or ATM/ Debit card to make your purchase online. Ironic, isn't it?

Finding mistakes on your credit report and what to do:

When you order your credit report, you will find a "Dispute Form" enclosed. The dispute form will ask you to identify the account/s you are disputing, company name, account number and the reason for the dispute. Examples: the account may not be yours; a collection account might show a paid account as not being paid in full, or that payment arrangements have been made; your personal information may be incorrect; a credit card account that you closed may appear as still being open, and many other possibilities. It is your responsibility to be sure that the information on the credit report is factually correct.

When disputing inaccurate information on your credit report, send the Dispute Form to the credit reporting agencies and the company that owns the account you are disputing. Send the Dispute Form by certified mail, return receipt requested. By law (The Fair Credit Reporting Act), a creditor and the agencies have a reasonable period of time (determined to be thirty business days) to investigate and resolve your dispute. Then, one of four things will happen. 1. The disputed information will confirm that the client is correct, at which time the information must be removed. 2. The dispute will be verified by the lender and remain on your credit report. 3. A "Statement of Dispute" will be added to your report and, if unresolved, remain on your report for seven years. 4. You receive no response at all. Never give up. Be persistent and start over if necessary. Keep accurate records of whom you speak with, proof of mailing (certified mail receipt), dates and times, and anything else that may be important and relevant. Be careful not to dispute any information that you know for a fact is correct, hoping the creditor will not respond within the thirty days. You just might wake up a giant or open up a big can of worms. In other words, if the information on your report is factual, there is nothing you can do to remove it, but you can explain it in a statement of up to 100 words, sent to the pertinent credit reporting agency.

Fraud Alerts- Obtain Free Copies Of All Three Credit Reports

It is extremely important that you protect your credit file. **Millions** of consumers had their identity stolen in 2004. To help keep your identity from being stolen and used, call **Equifax's** fraud alert number, **800-685-1111**. Equifax will in turn contact the other two agencies. With-in 7-10 days you will receive a simple form to complete from each agency. Fill out each form and return them to the appropriate agency. You will then be mailed your credit reports. This process will take approximately 7-10 days. The fraud alert will stay on your file for 90 days. Should you be a victim of fraud, the alert will remain on your files for one year. You will also be required to submit additional information regarding the crime. Please do not assume this is a fool proof solution. Ordering copies of your credit reports at least twice per year is also very important in the prevention of identity theft. Do not think this cannot happen to you. Another form of prevention is to purchase a "Credit Monitoring" program. There are a variety of these programs ranging in prices from $39.95-$79.95, depending on the different options and services offered. Money well spent! Banks are now offering the same services, but are normally more expensive.

Types Of Credit Reported To Credit Reporting Agencies

Mortgage Credit—Self explanatory. Your home. The collateral is your house.

Revolving Credit—This type of credit allows you to pay for all or part of your debt balance on a credit card. No collateral required.

Installment Loan—Examples of installment loans are a car, furniture, boat, appliances, education, etc. The terms of an installment loan require that you pay a specific amount of money and a specific monthly payment over a specific period of time. Collateral is required, usually—in most cases, the item purchased.

Open Charge Credit—30 to 90 days same as cash. This bill is due in full with no payment terms available. The item you purchased is usually the collateral.

Service Credit—Utilities, such as telephone, electricity, gas, water, cable T.V. Service credit requires payment in full for services used; no finance charges, but you could be charged a late fee if the bill is paid after the due date. The service may even be turned off if payment is not received. You will receive a notice that warns of a possible shut-off if payment is not received by the date written on the notice. Note: This type of account would only be reported to the credit reporting agency if you had an unsettled payment due and it was acquired by or sold to a collection agency.

At one time credit reports were used only for obtaining credit. Not any more. A prospective employer, a lender, your current employer, insurance companies, you as a customer. You apply for the dream job you have been searching and patiently waiting for. The employer asks permission to get a copy of your credit report. Why? Having negative entries on your credit report may alert the employer that you are not a "responsible" person based on that information. The employer may assume you will be late for work several times, call in sick frequently, take extra long breaks, or be less productive than other employees. This may be unfair, but it is legal. Anyone obtaining a credit report on you must have your permission to do so.

Credit Scoring

A credit score is a calculated number that lenders use to help them decide whether you are a great credit risk, good credit risk, fair credit risk, or a poor credit risk. Your credit score is a snapshot of your credit risk at a particular point in time. The most widely used credit bureau scores are based on a statistical model developed by Fair Isaac company. This is known as your FICO score. It is very possible, and more likely, that your FICO score will be the most important number you will have in the near future. Understanding credit scoring can help you manage your debt and credit. A FICO score looks at the same information in your credit report that a lender will also use. By knowing your FICO score and how your credit is evaluated, you can take actions that will lower your credit risk and raise your score over time.

Presently, FICO scores provide the best guide to future risk based solely on credit report data. The higher the score (maximum 850), the lower the credit risk. However, no score can predict whether a specific individual will be a good or bad customer. Each lender has its own strategy, including the level of risk it finds acceptable for a given credit product (automobile, mortgage, credit cards, appliances, etc.). There is no single cut-off score used by all lenders. Many lenders use the FICO score and also include their own scoring data. Lenders will include your income, how long you have worked at your present job, whether you have a phone in your name, whether you are self-employed or paid by commission, and several other factors that can go into qualifying you for the particular loan. Another scoring system you may be familiar with or heard of is a Beacon score. The FICO scoring system is more widely used.

FICO scores evaluate five main categories of information

1. Payment History

The first thing a lender wants to know is whether you have paid past credit accounts on time. This is the most important factor in computing a credit score. This information makes up approximately **35%** of your score. Do not assume that not having any late payments will give you a perfect score. Your payment history is only one piece of information used in calculating your score. Your score takes into account payment information on many types of accounts—VISA, MasterCard, Discover, American Express, retail accounts, installment loans, student loans, and others. Public record and collection accounts, bankruptcies, foreclosures, lawsuits, wage attachments, liens and judgements are also taken into account.

2. Amount Owed

Approximately **30%** of your score is based on the amount owed. Having credit accounts and owing money on them does not mean you are a high-risk borrower. However, owing large amounts on many accounts can indicate that you are overextended and living too much off credit cards, because of not having sufficient cash. If you are in this situation, it is more likely you will be late or not pay at all. Keep your credit balances at 20%, and no more than 40%, of your available credit. This will be a factor in your score. Paying off your credit card debts will improve your score over a period of time, normally 3-6 months.

3. Length of Credit History

Generally, a long credit history will increase your score, as long as the credit history is positive and what the rest of your credit report looks like. The score considers both the age of your oldest account and an average age of all your accounts, how long specific accounts have been established, and how long it has been since you have used certain accounts. Approximately **15%** of your score is based on this information.

4. Obtaining New Credit

Research shows that applying for or opening several new accounts in a short period of time represents a great risk. Remember that too many inquiries will also hurt your credit score. Typically, each time you initiate an inquiry (apply for credit cards or loans) your FICO score can go down 5-9 points. Note that if YOU order your credit report or a lender has made an inquiry to offer you credit or see whether you qualify for a pre-approved credit card offer. Neither will affect your FICO score. Both of these instances are not an indication that you are seeking additional credit. **10%** of your score is based on this category. Do not presume you will automatically receive a pre-approved credit card just because it says you are pre-approved. What is the first thing the issuer does when you accept the credit card offer? The lender reviews your most recent credit reports. There is no such thing as pre-approved, which is why many credit card companies are now using the term pre-selected.

5. Types of Credit In Use

Do you have a healthy mix of credit cards, retail accounts (department stores), and finance company accounts (installment loans)? It is not necessary to have one of each, and it is not a good idea to open credit accounts to improve your mix, or open accounts that you do not intend to use. Having too many accounts will have a negative effect on your FICO score, because lenders take a serious look at your "potential debt," as mentioned in an earlier chapter. **10%** is based on this category.

The Top Ten Reasons You May Be Denied Credit

1. Serious delinquency
2. Collection accounts
3. Derogatory public record
4. Time since the delinquency is too short or unknown.
5. Level of delinquency on accounts
6. Number of delinquent accounts
7. Amount owed on accounts
8. Proportion of balances to credit limits is too high.
9. Length of time accounts have been established
10. Too many accounts with balances

Tips For Raising Your FICO Score

Make sure your credit reports are correct. Get all three combined into a "merged report."

Pay bills on time (paying on time for 6 consecutive months could raise your FICO score by 20 points).

If you have missed payments, get current and do your very best to stay current.

If you are having trouble making ends meet, contact your creditors. They may be able to help.

Keep balances on credit cards low (20% and no more than 40% of available credit). More than 40% could affect your FICO score.

Pay down balances on your credit cards. (Paying down the debt by 34% could increase your FICO score by 20 points).

Pay off your debt rather than moving it around. Each balance transfer reduces your FICO score by three points.

The maximum FICO score you can obtain is 850. The national average is 680. In order to qualify for advertised "best deals" (No Money Down, 0% Interest, No Payment Until Years Later), your FICO score should be at least 720, but closer to 750.

Would you like to see where your credit score stands among the rest of U.S. consumers?

up to 499 = 1%
500-549 = 5%
550-599 = 7%
600-649 = 11%
650-699 = 16%
700-749 = 20%
750-799 = 29%
800 plus = 11%

Your goal should be to have a minimum FICO score of 680.

Please do not get discouraged if you have a low score. With patience, persistence, time, perseverance, and proper spending, YOU can and will increase your credit score.

NEVER GIVE UP
BELIEVE IN YOURSELF
WRITE DOWN YOUR FINANCIAL GOALS!

Read this book more than once. How important is a FINANCIAL PLAN, especially when it is YOUR FINANCIAL PLAN?

I have spent countless hours writing this book from my heart. I truly hope the information helps make a tremendous impact on your life. It will, if you take action with your finances.

Summary Questions For Chapter 6

All of the following are credit reporting agencies except,
A. TransUnion
B. Equifax
C. TWA
D. Experian

All 3 credit reporting agencies receive and report the same information.
A. True
B. False

This type of information is reported to all 3 credit reporting agencies, except:
A. Payment history
B. Race
C. Collection accounts
D. Social Security number

_____ makes up 35% of your FICO score.
A. Credit mix
B. Amount owed
C. Obtaining new credit
D. Payment history

Name two reasons you could be denied credit.
_____
_____

Name two ways to increase your FICO score.
_____
_____

The national average FICO score is:
A. 550
B. 680
C. 750
D. 640

_____ % **Of consumers have a FICO score over 700-750.**

Name two types of credit reported to credit reporting agencies.

_____

_____

Lenders report all account information to each of the three credit reporting agencies.
A. True
B. False

Chapter 7—Types of Spenders

Which Buying Categories Do You Fall Into?

The Co-dependent Spender

The co-dependent spender attempts to instill dependency in others by showering them with perceived necessities, such as clothing, jewelry, the latest technology products, computers, televisions, CD players, and much more.

The Narcissistic Spender

The narcissistic spender, in order to overcome the lack of self-esteem and feelings of inner inferiority, spends money by making purchases to look good. This type of spender buys designer clothing, hair and skin treatments, and products that signify status, such as expensive watches and jewelry.

The Compulsive Spender

The compulsive spender has a feeling of inner emptiness and buys things as a quick-fix in order to feel better. Even though the goal of making yourself feel better is normally temporary, compulsive spenders go binge shopping and spend frivolously.

The Revengeful Spender

A revenge spender wants to punish someone (normally a spouse or significant other) by spending their money. In a way, this spender steals the money right from out of their pocket, a credit card, or directly from the bank.

The emotions behind various spending patterns can be the reasons that well-intentioned, intelligent individuals continually spend more than they earn. Another factor is that we were raised with different perceptions of money. Some of us were taught that money (actually the love of money) is the root of all evil, as we listened to stories that ended in tragedy. These stories and beliefs shape children's perceptions of money. Should we fear money or embrace it? Is spending and having money a symbol of power? **We need to understand that money's true power is in the realization that it can create financial freedom.**

Types Of Delinquent Debtors

Before discussing different types of debtors, I would like to reinforce the fact that we all have choices. Your choices result from the decisions you have made, not anyone else. As I have said many times, **we must learn to say NO to ourselves more often.** You must question whether the choices you make and have made are in the best interest of **yourself and your family**.

The Impulsive

Impulsive buyers, for whatever emotional reason, knowingly spend more money than they have. Often they have an inability to say no to salespeople, or they spend money on friends in order to earn acceptance and be liked.

The Imprudent

These consumers do not have two nickels to rub together in savings for a rainy day or an unexpected emergency. They have no financial goals and live one day at a time. Soon looking in the mirror, they are now at retirement age and cannot understand where the time has gone. Members of this group have many problems with stress, unstable relationships, anxiety, lack of productivity, and they are one disaster or unexpected emergency away from financial ruin.

The Unethical

These consumers borrow money on credit with no intention of ever repaying their loans. Instead, other consumers are the ones who make their payments in the form of higher interest rates and increased costs for services and products purchased.

The Naive

It's hard to believe, but some consumers feel that if they just ignore their debt, it will magically disappear...honest! The only thing that is actually disappearing is their chance for any kind of financial freedom. Please do not ignore debt; confront it.

The Impoverished

From time to time, a high-risk consumer will be mistakenly issued a credit card. Then this consumer uses it to purchase essential items, such as food, clothing and shelter. Now along with the cost of the purchase, they must also deal with the added cost of finance charges.

The Victim of Fortune

I am sure we have all heard the saying that "bad things happen to good people." Many consumers do everything right: They have a plan, they save, and they are very responsible when it comes to borrowing and spending. Due to some catastrophic life event, such as an extended illness, loss of a beloved family member, being downsized by their employer, an accident or disability, they suffer financial collapse. Life is not always fair, but being overwhelmed with debt can and often happens to conscientious, money-savvy people.

Food For Thought

Instead of asking you summary questions at the end of this chapter, I will discuss attitudes, beliefs, and actions. I bet you have heard this on more than one occasion—"been there, done that." Well, early on, I told you that I have fallen flat on my face more than once. The hardest thing to do is get up, brush yourself off, and continue doing the very best you can. Sometimes that is easier said than done, I know that, **but you can, and more importantly, must!** There are no free lunches and the times we live in have certainly changed drastically from the previous generation.

Do not let life pass you by—it will if YOU let it. Choices are not inherited; they are actions and decisions you make that affect either your failure or success (achievement). I realize, sadly, that many of you will skim through this book and forget about it. Others will read it and cannot wait to start taking control of their finances, only to see their enthusiasm fade with time. The most successful of you will read this book, implement the changes and continue maintaining your commitment and sincere desire to make a positive difference in your financial life. You must have more than just willpower. Willpower is not enough by itself, and will eventually fade with time. I stand by my word that the information contained in this book will make a tremendous difference in your life. And remember, it is strictly up to you. Be patient. This is not a get-rich-quick process, but in relation to the time you will be living, it is like a blink of an eye. We are not talking about losing weight, exercising, creating great abs, or improving your appearance. We are talking about the type of lifestyle you want for yourself and for your family, that is, having enough money to provide yourself with what you want and need, and enjoying your retirement years with dignity and independence.

The following are words of wisdom about making the right choices. There is no magic involved. I do not own a mysterious, magical tree in the backyard that grows money to share with all of you. I wish I did!

- **Believe in yourself and exude confidence.**
- **Write down your goals: personal, spiritual, family, and financial.**
- **Never give up. Successful people are the ones who do things others are not willing to do.**
- **We are where we are. Forget about the past and go forward.**
- **PLEASE complete the goals, budgeting worksheet and the other assignments.**
- **Always treat people the way you would like to be treated. It seems that the words or phrases "please, thank you, no sir, yes ma'am, excuse me" have vanished over time. They are important. Let's bring them back.**
- **Compliment someone everyday. What goes around comes around.**
- **Respect one another. Let others know how much you appreciate them.**
- **Have a burning, sincere desire to succeed.**
- **Create a specific game plan and be committed to it.**
- **Stay away from people who try to belittle your ambitions, dreams and goals.**

- Surround yourself with positive thinking people. Be a positive influence, yourself.

- Always do the best you can and DARE to DREAM!

- Learn to listen effectively.

- Do not be afraid to ask questions. There are NO stupid questions.

- Teach your children about finances. Give them this book to read and study.

- Be loyal, whether to a friend, your employer—even an acquaintance.

- Help someone less fortunate than yourself.

- THINK about the choices you make and their potential effect before following through.

- Do not try to keep up with the Jonses. Material things are not the definition of success or happiness.

- Be thankful. Everyday we talk to individuals who are in a much worse situation than you are. Just look around.

- Write down and discuss your VALUES with your family members. Is it your family, job, security, independence, success?

- Knowledge is power, but without action, it is just a word.

From personal experience, I know that implementing these suggestions will open so many doors of opportunity for you, and also give you a feeling of euphoria. If you want something badly enough, and if you are willing to be committed and make some sacrifices in your lifestyle and priorities, and changes in your thinking, you are there—wherever and whatever it is you want to be. There are no limitations on what you can accomplish, other than the limitations you put on yourself.

Once again, I would like to wish you the very best on your exciting journey to becoming debt-free. Hang on, because it will be a journey filled with tremendous successes and occasional hurdles to overcome. If it were easy, anyone could do it and you are not just anyone! Right?

BUDGETING WORKSHEET
Please Photocopy For Future Use

Monthly Income	Target Amount	Month	Month	Month	Month	Total Month __ to __
Salary/Wages	$	$	$	$	$	$
Salary/Wages (spouse)	$	$	$	$	$	$
Alimony/child support	$	$	$	$	$	$
Dividends (Investments)	$	$	$	$	$	$
Interest Income	$	$	$	$	$	$
Military pay	$	$	$	$	$	$
Pension Plan/Retirement	$	$	$	$	$	$
Rent Estate (Rent)	$	$	$	$	$	$
Royalties/Other Income	$	$	$	$	$	$
Social Security	$	$	$	$	$	$
Unemployment/Food Stamps	$	$	$	$	$	$
TOTAL INCOME	$	$	$	$	$	$

LIVING EXPENSES						
Food (Home, Work, School)	$	$	$	$	$	$
Electric/Gas/Oil	$	$	$	$	$	$
Water/Trash	$	$	$	$	$	$
Cable TV/Satellite	$	$	$	$	$	$
Telephone (Home, Cell, Internet)	$	$	$	$	$	$
Alimony/Child support	$	$	$	$	$	$
Child Care	$	$	$	$	$	$
Children Activities	$	$	$	$	$	$
Clothing	$	$	$	$	$	$
Contributions/Donations	$	$	$	$	$	$
Auto Gas/Maintenance	$	$	$	$	$	$
Auto Insurance	$	$	$	$	$	$
Health and Dental Insurance	$	$	$	$	$	$
Homeowners/Renters Insurance	$	$	$	$	$	$
Education (Tuition, Supplies)	$	$	$	$	$	$
Personal Care (Hair, Nails)	$	$	$	$	$	$
Medical Care (Prescriptions)	$	$	$	$	$	$
Laundry/Dry Cleaning	$	$	$	$	$	$
Household Items	$	$	$	$	$	$

Alarm Service	$	$	$	$	$	$
Gardner, Pool Service	$	$	$	$	$	$
Homeowners Dues	$	$	$	$	$	$
Subscription/Gym	$	$	$	$	$	$
Membership	$	$	$	$	$	$

SECURED/UNSECURED DEBTS						
Rent/Mortgage (1st & 2nd)	$	$	$	$	$	$
Auto Loans/Leases	$	$	$	$	$	$
Personal Loans	$	$	$	$	$	$
Student Loans	$	$	$	$	$	$
Recreation Toys (Watercraft, etc.)	$	$	$	$	$	$
Credit Cards	$	$	$	$	$	$
Medical Bills	$	$	$	$	$	$
Trailer Park Space Rent	$	$	$	$	$	$
Other Expenses or Debts	$	$	$	$	$	$
TOTAL EXPENSES	$	$	$	$	$	$

MONTHLY CASH FLOW						
Total Income	$	$	$	$	$	$
Total Expenses	$	$	$	$	$	$
Disposable Income/Deficit	$	$	$	$	$	$

CREDITOR SUMMARY

NO.	CREDITOR NAME	ACCOUNT NUMBER	BALANCE	MINIMUM MO. PAYMENT	INTEREST RATE	DATE LAST PAID
1			$	$	%	
2			$	$	%	
3			$	$	%	
4			$	$	%	
5			$	$	%	
6			$	$	%	
7			$	$	%	
8			$	$	%	
9			$	$	%	
10			$	$	%	
11			$	$	%	
12			$	$	%	
13			$	$	%	
14			$	$	%	
15			$	$	%	
16			$	$	%	
17			$	$	%	
18			$	$	%	
19			$	$	%	
20			$	$	%	

Summary of Budget

Total Net Income	$
	(Minus)
Total Living Expenses Payments	$
Total Secured Debt Payments	$
Total Unsecured Debt Payments	$
Deficit Income	$

Note: If you have ended up with a deficit you should seriously consider a reputable credit counseling /debt management organization to help reduce your expenses.

FINANCIAL GOALS & DEBT-TO-INCOME RATIO
Please Photocopy this sheet for future use

Short-term Goals-less than 1 year

My Specific Goal	Total Cost of Your Goal	Number of months to reach your Goal	Amount Needed to Save Each Month For your Goal
1.	$		$
2.	$		$
3.	$		$
4.	$		$
5.	$		$

Mid-term Goals-Between 1 to 5 years

My Specific Goal	Total Cost of Your Goal	Number of months to reach your Goal	Amount Needed to Save Each Month For your Goal
1.	$		$
2.	$		$
3.	$		$
4.	$		$
5.	$		$

Long-term Goals-Over 5 years

My Specific Goal	Total Cost of Your Goal	Number of months to reach your Goal	Amount Needed to Save Each Month For your Goal
1.	$		$
2.	$		$
3.	$		$
4.	$		$
5.	$		$

Debt to Income Calculation

$(Debt) Divided by $ (Income) = _____ %

How Lenders View Your Credit Worthiness

Debt-to-Income Ratio	(Less than 10%)	Excellent
Debt-to-Income Ratio	(10% to 20%)	Very Good
Debt-to-Income Ratio	(20% to 35%)	Fair
Debt-to-Income Ratio	(35% and Higher)	High Risk

Paying Bills and Money Saving Worksheet
Please Photocopy This Sheet For Future Use

Due Dates – 1ˢᵗ to 15ᵗʰ

Bills To Pay	Due Date	Payment	Bills To Pay	Due Date	Payment
1.		$	8.		$
2.		$	9		$
3.		$	10.		$
4.		$	11.		$
5.		$	12		$
6.		$	13.		$
7.		$	Total Monthly Payment Due 1ˢᵗ – 15ᵗʰ$		$

Due Dates – 15ᵗʰ to 31ˢᵗ

Bills To Pay	Due Date	Payment	Bills To Pay	Due Date	Payment
1.		$	8.		$
2.		$	9		$
3.		$	10.		$
4.		$	11.		$
5.		$	12		$
6.		$	13.		$
7.		$	Total Monthly Payment Due 15ᵗʰ – 31ˢᵗ		$

Bill Paying & Money Saving Calculations

$_____ (Minus) $_____ (Equals) $_____

Total Monthly Net   Total Monthly   Total Disposable
Take Home Income   Bills To Pay   Income

Note: Take your "Total Disposable Income" and divide it up into the three accounts below.

$_____ $_____ $_____

Entertainment   Saving   Emergency
Account   Account   Account

(Goal 5 %)   (Goal 10 %)   (Goal 5 %)

Pathway To Financial Success. Suggested Financial Goals.

It is impossible to achieve financial wellness without a destination in mind. You cannot know where you are going or if you have already been there, unless you have a definable destination. Developing financial goals is crucial and requires proper planning. You must have patience, discipline, and a sincere willingness and desire to accomplish your financial goals. Having financial peace of mind and control of your finances requires lifestyle changes, thinking changes, priority changes and most importantly, proper financial planning and a sincere desire to make appropriate changes. Poor spending habits, regardless of your income, can almost guarantee accruing overwhelming debt. Some very difficult sacrifices and work will be required.

1. Determine a specific goal you want to accomplish. Stay unswervingly dedicated to achieving each goal.

2. Develop a specific game plan to achieve your goals. Determine the timeframe to complete each goal.

3. Have a sincere burning desire to attain the things you want in life—nothing less! There is a big difference between a goal and a wish. Recognize the difference, but please remember your opportunities are endless.

4. Develop extreme confidence about yourself and your abilities. Do not accept the possibility of defeat. Never give up! Concentrate only on the positive and your strengths.

5. Do not allow criticism, what others might say, circumstances, or any obstacles affect your dogged determination to succeed. Do not allow anyone rain on your parade to a better financial destination.

I cannot stress enough the importance of setting goals for getting where you want to be. Reading how to do this is not going to be as easy as taking action. I promise you, continuously applying these steps will become second nature to you. Action and consistency will create the desired results. Your financial situation WILL change for the better. Over time, correctly managing your finances will become exciting, as you create a bright future. Seeing the light at the end of the tunnel is strictly up to you. Remember, YOU CAN DO THIS! I wish you could see through our eyes, the great things awaiting you.

<u>START NOW</u> and create "Your Personal Success Plan."

- Keep track of every penny you spend for a minimum of 1- 3 months.
- Order copies of your credit reports). Twice per year.
- Dispute incorrect information.
- Protect yourself against identity theft.
- Negotiate reducing your credit card interest rates.
- Eliminate your credit card debt.
- Prepare a budget.
- Calculate your debt-to-income-ratio
- Contribute more to your company sponsored retirement plan.
- Start a savings plan.
- Create a total game plan for yourself.
- Dare to dream.
- Believe in yourself!

Important and Useful Web Sites

Bankruptcy
www.usdoj.gov/ust
www.abiworld.org
www.ftc.gov

Career Development
www.careerbuilder.com
www.getajobservices.com
www.one-to-one-coach, com
www.jobweb.com
www.rpi.edu
www.bridgewaycareer. com

Child Support Enforcement
www.acf.dhhs.gov

Consumer Action
(415)-777-9365   (Consumer Complaint Hotline)
(213)-624-8327   (General Hotline)

Consumer Action Handbook-Please order this FREE book.
www.consumeraction.gov

Consumer Information Center
http://www.gsa.gov:807staff/pa/cic/cic/html

Credit Card Fraud Prevention
http://epn.com/bha
http://ftc.gov

Credit Issues and Statute Of Limitations for Each State

http://www.cardreport.com/laws

Credit Reports and Scoring

www.experian.com
www.equifax.com
www.transunion.com
www.myfico.com
www.fairisaac.com
www.acb-credit. com

Credit Reports Free/No Hidden Agenda/No Obligation

www.annualcreditreport.com (availability depends on the state you live in)

Fathers' Rights

www.dadsrights.com

Federal Trade Commission (FTC)

www.ftc.com

Housing Counseling (list of agencies)

www.hud.gov/hsg/sfh/hee/hee/heeprofl4.cfm

How To Resolve Your Consumer Complaint

http://seamless.com/talf/tx/intro.html

Marriage Counseling

www.divorcestopper.com
www.marriagesolutions.org
www.marriagematters.com
www.marriagesuccess.com
www.abuse-recovery-and-marriage-counseling.com

Mortgages and Refinancing

www.mbaa.org

Mortgage Information and Calculator

www.irwinmortgage.com

www.hud.gov

Problems Making Mortgage Payments-Near Foreclosure

www.homesaversusa.com

Real Estate Relocation

www.homefair.com

Renters' Rights

www.renters-rights.com   www.nolo.com

www.onlinelegalcenter.com

Student Loans

www.loanconsolidation.ed.gov

www.estudentloan.com

www.credittalk.com

www.studentmarket.com

www.salliemae.com

www.fastweb.com

www.youngmoney.com

http://www.financial-education-icfe.org

Money Saving Strategies And More

Do you have a mortgage funded by the VA or FHA?

The FHA and VA have a refinance plan called "The Streamline Loan or The Mortgage Modification Loan". With this program, there is no income verification or credit check required. You will normally have three different options to choose from ranging in cost, depending on the interest rate you choose. If you plan on staying in the home for more than three years, take any closing costs and add that into the mortgage so that you have very little, if any out of pocket expense. Call your mortgage lender and ask for a Senior Loan Representative, as many people working for the lender are unaware of this type of refinance program.

Are you paying PMI insurance each month?

Mortgage lenders have a monthly charge referred to as "PMI" insurance, which protects the bank should a customer file bankruptcy. Private Mortgage Insurance is required to be paid, if you have less than 20% equity in your property. The equity does not have to consist of cash payments, but also includes appreciation. Under normal circumstances, your property will appreciate 7%-10% per year. Contact your mortgage lender to inquire whether you have the 20% equity required to eliminate PMI insurance, which can be a substantial cost each month. The lender may require that you have an appraisal of the property completed, which normally costs $200.00-$300.00. The lender will normally require that you use their appraiser.

Taxes!

Many people assume the number of allowances you claim on your W-4 is directly related to the number of dependents you have, which is incorrect. The number of allowances you claim on your W-4 is dependent on tax deductible expenses, such as deductible mortgage interest, deductible IRA's, small business expenses, to name a few. This may be the cause of receiving a substantial refund from the Internal Revenue Service. How much interest do you earn on that money you overpay in taxes? That is right, 0%. Check with a tax expert or your employer's payroll department to determine the correct number of allowances you should claim to increase your monthly income. Keep in mind, that if you adjust your allowances, you will no longer receive a large refund check and be careful not to claim too many allowances, as you do not want to owe any monies to the IRS at the end of the year.

Make a specific list when grocery shopping.

Never shop when you are hungry. You will notice a sizeable difference in your grocery bill. Make a list of exactly what you intend to purchase and approximate cost of your total list. Take $5.00 - $10.00 as a buffer. DO NOT take your credit cards including your debit card. Get into the habit of using cash only. Have you ever gone into a store for a gallon of milk and ended up leaving with $50.00 - $100.00 worth of groceries? Remember, 65% of all purchases we make are unplanned!

Use grocery coupons.

Every Sunday after church my wife and I spend about ½ hour cutting out grocery coupons. Each month we save $30.00 - $50.00. Not bad for a ½ hour worth of work. Using store brands can also save you a substantial amount of money.

Shop your Homeowners & Automobile at least once every two years. Last year we saved $600.00.. .$50.00 a month and increased our coverages. Consider increasing deductibles

Save at least $1.00 per day

Each and every day, save one dollar and put it into a piggy bank or container of some kind. Along with that strategy, when you make any kind of purchase, use cash only. At the end of the day put the change in with your dollar bills. Even if you only saved $30.00 per month @ 10% over 40 years is equal to almost $70,000.00. Just pocket change!

Wait for sales!

Comparison shopping will save you as much as 50% of the original purchase price. I have paid $50.00 for something my wife found at half the price just by comparison shopping. All that is required is a little more of your time.

Identity Theft

This may not save you any money, but will help you keep it. Here are the numbers for **The Credit Reporting Agencies Fraud Alert System**. Anytime you apply for a loan or use a credit card differently than you normally do: for example, you have always used your credit card to purchase gasoline and then there is a purchase for a big screen television. Anytime you take out a loan or the normal use of your card has changed, you will be contacted to make sure it was you who actually made the purchase. There is NO COST for this service.

EXPERIAN   1 (888) 397-3742
EQUIFAX   1 (800) 525-6285
TRANSUNION   1 (800) 680-7249

OPT OUT OPTION

Tired of getting all those credit card offers. This will stop the credit card offers from coming and help you avoid the temptation of adding to your debt. You can choose not receiving anymore offers for two years or ten years at NO COST. 1 (888) 567-8688

Garage and yard sales

Have you had a garage or yard sale recently? You would be surprised what many people consider a real find and are willing to pay money for. Take a thorough tour around your home or apartment. Finding things that you forgot you had or do no not use anymore? Are they taking up space and collecting dust? Turn those items into cash! You may have hundreds of dollars worth of items that you may think is junk, and others would consider treasure.

Special Thanks To Some Very Special People In My Life

I am very blessed to have several colleques, friends and especially my family help to make one of my dreams and goals a reality. They have all played a big role in helping me live my dream. Making a positive difference in people's lives, as many of them have.

My wife, Janet S. Kenworthy who has made a tremendous difference in my life. Thanks for always being by my side and believing in me. I could not have done this without your help and endless devotion. I love you very much.

My son and daughter, Steven M. Kenworthy and Samantha S. Thornton. The best of the best. I am so proud of both of you. I am the luckiest father in the world! Lots of love, Dad :o).

My wonderful grandchildren who keep me going 100 miles per hour. Josephine Thornton, Reagan Thornton, Nicholas McKnight, Lucas McKnight and Jacob Bauer.

My father & mother Gregory M. Kenworthy and Laura A. Kenworthy, who helped me develop into the person I am. Thanks from my heart. Love you both.

My brother and his wife, Jeffrey M. Kenworthy and Dora Kenworthy. Thank you very much for your continuous support and unconditional love. Back at you one hundred fold. Love ya!

Thanks to my youngest sister Kelly Spicher, her husband Doug and their children, Kyle and Cameren Spicher.

Kim Hafner, my sister's husband who went above and beyond to make Jackie's life a happy one. Most husbands would have given up. Thank you, thank you, thank you! You are an amazing man.

Mr. & Mrs. Sal and Dottie Curto, business officers for TAG. Thank you for opening up so many doors of opportunity for me. You are both fantastic people.

Thomas Roland, President of ElimiDebt, who also believed in me. Thank you for the chance to make a difference in so many people's lives.

Warren Carlson, a dear friend who did an outstanding job editing my book. Your efforts are greatly appreciated. Thanks very much.

Michael Martone, whose years of friendship, business ideas, professionalism and expertise were and are an inspiration.

Lori Pingley. A miracle worker who took my photograph for the book. Lori also professionally designed the book cover. Thank you for the awesome job and your hard work.

Last, but certainly not least, my friend and partner, Perry Kerney Sr. I cannot put into words the tremendous difference you have made in my life. Thank you for your wisdom, beliefs, knowledge, and empowering me to get back on course with my passion of helping people, regardless of any obstacles. Together, there are no limits as to what we can and will accomplish.

www.ingramcontent.com/pod-product-compliance
Lightning Source LLC
Chambersburg PA
CBHW022023170526
45157CB00003B/1337